IN THE AMERICAN WEST

ANDY WILKINSON, SERIES EDITOR

ALSO IN THIS SERIES:

Bad Smoke, Good Smoke: A Rancher's View of Texas Wildfire
by John R. Erickson

Cowboy's Lament: A Life on the Open Range
by Frank Maynard; edited by Jim Hoy

The Hell-Bound Train: A Cowboy Songbook, Second Edition
by Glenn Ohrlin; edited by Charlie Seemann

If I Was a Highway
by Michael Ventura

In My Father's House: A Memoir of Polygamy
by Dorothy Allred Solomon

Llano Estacado: An Island in the Sky
Stephen Bogener and William Tydeman, editors

Light in the Trees
by Gail Folkins

On Becoming Apache
by Harry Mithlo and Conger Beasley Jr.

Rightful Place
by Amy Hale Auker

A Sweet Separate Intimacy: Women Writers of the American Frontier, 1800–1922
Susan Cummins Miller, editor

Texas Dance Halls: A Two-Step Circuit
by Gail Folkins and J. Marcus Weekley

TEXAS RED

RED STEAGALL

WITH JIM JENNINGS

TEXAS TECH UNIVERSITY PRESS

This book is typeset in EB Garamond. The paper used in this book meets the minimum requirements of ANSI/NISO Z39.48-1992 (R1997). ♾

Designed by Hannah Gaskamp
Cover design by Hannah Gaskamp
Front cover portrait by Mark Kohler, from a photo by Craig Swancy.

Library of Congress Cataloging-in-Publication Data

Names: Steagall, Red, author. | Jennings, Jim (James N.) contributor. | McEntire, Reba, writer of foreword. Title: Texas Red / by Red Steagall, with Jim Jennings; foreword by Reba McEntire.
Description: Lubbock: Texas Tech University Press, 2024. | Series: Voice in the American West | Summary: "An essential Western autobiography of Red Steagall, a beloved American cowboy poet"—Provided by publisher.
Identifiers: LCCN 2024039587 | ISBN 978-1-68283-225-7 (cloth)
Subjects: LCSH: Steagall, Red. | Country musicians—United States—Biography. | Cowboys—United States—Biography. | Poets—United States—Biography. | LCGFT: Autobiographies.
Classification: LCC ML420.S8155 A3 2024 | DDC 782.421642092 [B]—dc23/eng/20230828
LC record available at https://lccn.loc.gov/2024039587

Printed in the United States of America
24 25 26 27 28 29 30 31 32 / 9 8 7 6 5 4 3 2 1

Texas Tech University Press
Box 41037
Lubbock, Texas 79409-1037 USA
800.832.4042
ttup@ttu.edu
www.ttupress.org

This book is dedicated to my lifelong partner, my soulmate,
my very best friend and my most constructive critic,
my darling wife, Rita Gail Steagall.

I honestly believe that fifty years from now, the only way people will have a real idea of how we lived is from the things we write and record today. We must do it authentically, because what we say becomes the gospel.

—RED STEAGALL

CONTENTS

ILLUSTRATIONS

All photos credited to the Steagall Family Archives except as noted in the captions.

FOREWORD

If you are blessed enough in your lifetime to meet a person who will stand by you through thick and thin, guide you, share their wisdom, and always have your best interest at heart, then thank God for them every day.

Red Steagall is that kind of person. He's loyal, loving, and giving. He can tell the funniest joke; recite the most emotional, heartfelt poem; and voice the history of our country in a song. By the time he's through, you are standing with your hand over your heart, singing the National Anthem.

I would call Red a national treasure. I would call him a humanitarian and a loyal American. But best of all, I get to call him my friend, and I pray forever that he calls me his.

You will find out in this book how long Red has been singing and writing songs. You will find out how many miles he's traveled on horseback, in his buses, trucks, and cars to get to performances that he's worked so hard to make happen.

My wish for you is that one day you get to meet Red in person. If you do, you will never forget that meeting. I never have. I remember like it was yesterday when I first met Red. We were at the National Finals Rodeo, December 1974, in Oklahoma City. Little did I know then that we would become lifelong friends.

Thank you, Lord. I am so grateful.

Now, sit back, relax, and enjoy my friend's life story.

LOVE,
REBA MCENTIRE

TEXAS RED

CHAPTER 1

BEGINNINGS

I always wanted to be a cowboy. From my earliest memories, that's all I ever thought of. There were no cowboys in my family, and I didn't have a cowboy in particular to look up to, but I think growing up in a small Texas Panhandle town and being exposed to the outdoors probably put that idea in my mind.

My father roped calves when he was young, but he didn't make a living as a cowboy. This was a time when every little town in that part of the country had a roping arena, and lots of the local men would gather there a couple of nights a week to visit and rope. The men in my family were all farmers, merchants, and construction workers. When I was born, my parents lived about twenty-five miles from what had been the Chisholm Trail, the most famous cattle trail in history, over which five million head of cattle were driven by cowboys on their way to Kansas railheads. Probably no one in my family was even aware of that. They had no interest in it and were too busy trying to make a living.

I was born Russell Don Steagall in Gainesville, Texas, on December 22, 1938, near the end of the Great Depression. My mother and most of my immediate family called me Russell, but to everyone else, I was Red, owing to my bright red hair. My red hair has turned gray now, but I'm still Red.

My father, George Russell Steagall, was a truck driver for the Works Progress Administration (WPA), a government program created by President Franklin Roosevelt in 1935 to put people to work. There were 3.3 million Americans

My beautiful mother, the late Juanita Ruth Mitchell Steagall Robertson.

working for the WPA the year I was born. My mother, Juanita Ruth Steagall, was an elementary school teacher. We lived in Forestburg, Texas, a small community in Montague County, that, although there were only about 150 people living there, supported eight businesses, including a sawmill and a cotton gin.

My dad, the late George Russell Steagall, holding me shortly after my birth.

There was, however, no hospital, so when Mother told Daddy it was time for me to be born, he drove her the thirty miles into Gainesville, which had the nearest hospital. My brother, Carroll, was also born there.

Montague County is in North Texas, with its northern border being the Red River, that sometimes dry, sometimes flooded stream that separates Texas from Oklahoma. It's interesting that both sides of my family ended up in Montague County because they all had their origins in other places.

The Steagalls were one of the first families to settle in this country. William Steggall (the spelling was changed to Steagall in the next generation on my side of the family) was from Northern Ireland, but in 1635, for some unknown reason, he sailed to America from Liverpool, England, on the ship *The Plain Joane*. The ship docked at Jamestown, on the James River, in what became Virginia.

Jamestown was the first permanent English settlement in North America, having been founded in 1607, primarily by those seeking to avoid religious persecution in England, and it's possible that William went there for that reason. But the village's history up to 1635 had not been all that pleasant. Jamestown had gone through what is referred to as "the starving time," when almost everyone died of starvation, and there had been numerous Indian attacks. But William survived, married, and had five children.

Probably in the latter 1630s, William and his family moved to nearby Middle Plantation, which was a new settlement only about seven miles from Jamestown. Middle Plantation later became Williamsburg, which became the capital of the Virginia Colony. William is credited as being one of the founders of Williamsburg, Virginia.

William's descendants spread out through Virginia as the East Coast became more settled, and then into North Carolina and Tennessee. It was to Tennessee that my ancestors migrated.

In 1861, when the American Civil War—or the War of Northern Aggression, as my family calls it—broke out, the strategic importance of Tennessee became well known. More than 100,000 of its men joined the Confederate Army. My great-grandfather, George Henry Steagall, enlisted in the 35th Tennessee Infantry Regiment as a private and participated in some of the major battles of the war, including Shiloh, Chickamauga, and Atlanta, and was discharged as a sergeant at the end of the war in 1865. In 1870, George Henry, his wife Margaret, and his parents—my great-great-grandparents, Thomas Gardner Steagall Sr. and his wife Elizabeth—moved to Texas, settling in Grayson County.

Grayson County, like Montague County, had the Red River as its northern border. It became a major destination for immigrants bound for Texas, as many followed what was known as Preston Road, sometimes called the Shawnee Trail, down through Indian Territory—what became Oklahoma—into Texas. In one six-week period in 1845, roughly a thousand wagons crossed the river out of Indian Territory into Grayson County. By the mid-1850s, most of the population of Grayson County was from other southern states.

In 1877, my grandfather, Henry Berryman Steagall, was born in Grayson County, making him the first Steagall born in Texas. He married Dora Ethel Allen, who was born in 1882 in Mississippi before her family migrated to Texas. Her father, Russell Jefferson Allen, had been a postmaster for the Confederacy during the war.

By the early 1900s, my grandfather Henry and his wife Ethel had moved to Forestburg in Montague County, where they operated a grocery store. My father, George Russell Steagall, was born there in 1910, but when he entered high school, his family moved to nearby Nocona because my grandmother, Ethel, wanted my father to attend a larger school than what Forestburg had to offer. Both my grandfather and my father worked as butchers in a large grocery store in Nocona, but when my father graduated from high school in 1930, they moved back to Forestburg and opened another grocery store.

Forestburg, at that time, consisted of one city block, and every business in town was on that block. My grandfather's grocery store was at one end of the block, and there was another grocery store at the other end of the block. It was owned by my uncle, Meb Dunn.

My mother's family also came from Virginia. Her name was Juanita Ruth Mitchell, and her third great-grandfather was Joab Mitchell, who was born in Virginia in 1721. He married Mary Henderson, whose brother Richard Henderson owned the Transylvania Company of Kentucky. The Transylvania Company bought from the Cherokee Indians what are now the central and western parts of Kentucky, along with a pretty good-sized chunk of north central Tennessee. Joab went to work for his brother-in-law, and when Henderson hired Daniel Boone to establish the Wilderness Road going through the Cumberland Gap and into southeastern Kentucky, Joab went with him. He helped Boone build Fort Boonesborough, and he was killed there by Indians in 1780.

When I filmed a TV show at Boonesborough in 2017, it made the hair stand up on the back of my neck to walk through those grounds and realize that my fourth great-grandfather had fought and died in that very place.

Joab's sons, after the death of their father, moved into Tennessee, but my great-grandfather, Wiley Mitchell, left Tennessee and moved to Arkansas, which is where my grandfather, Robert Fain Mitchell, was born. But it seems like they all just kept moving west, and in the late 1800s, my grandfather Mitchell moved to Grayson County, Texas, and from there to Dye Mound in Montague County, where he married my grandmother, Mabel Ruth Hedgpeth.

Grandmother Hedgpeth was born in the Dixie community of Montague County in 1891, between the towns of Nocona and Montague. The Hedgpeths were originally from Lincoln County, Tennessee, near Fayetteville, but Grandmother's father and mother, John Seamon Hedgpeth and his wife Sinah, had lived in Arkansas before they migrated to Texas and ended up in Montague County.

Mother was born in 1917 in Ringgold, Texas, which is also in Montague County, but when she was 5, her family moved twenty miles east to Bonita, which is just east of Nocona. My grandfather Mitchell was a farmer—most everyone was at that time—and he was raising various grains, probably wheat and oats. But cotton had become the big thing, and it appeared to him that the farmers who were growing cotton were getting rich. However, Ringgold was so close to the Red River that the soil in that river bottom was too tight for cotton. He sold that farm, bought another near Bonita, and started raising cotton.

After Mother graduated from high school, she attended North Texas State Teachers College in Denton, and in two years received a teaching certificate. Her first teaching job was in Forestburg, where she rented a room from Ethel and Henry Steagall. That, of course, is how she met their son, George. George and Ruth were married in January 1938. He was 27; she was 20.

Even after the Depression ended and the country began to get back on its feet, the government kept the WPA going, and Daddy continued to work for the program. But by early 1941, with the war in Europe heating up, there were better jobs coming available. My uncle, Johnny Miller, Mother's oldest sister's husband, had found a job in Sanford, Texas, which was north of Amarillo, up on the Canadian River in the Texas Panhandle. He was working for a natural gas company, and he let Daddy know that there was opportunity for work there. So, we loaded up everything we owned, which wasn't much, and moved to Sanford. I was 3 years old; my brother Carroll was still a toddler, and my brother Barry was a baby.

Sanford was very small, and it was overshadowed by the largest town in the upper Texas Panhandle, Borger. Oil had been discovered in the north central Panhandle in 1926, and Borger sprang up overnight. Within a short time, what had been open prairie had become a city with a population of 45,000. In the months that followed, oilmen, roughnecks, prospectors, panhandlers, and fortune seekers were joined in the town by card sharks, prostitutes, bootleggers, and drug dealers. Borger became so notorious that in the spring of 1927, Texas governor Dan Moody sent a force of Texas Rangers to rein in the town. Borger was referred to as "Borger by day, and a booger by night."

About twelve miles to the west of Borger, a large natural gas field was discovered in 1926. On top of it, the town of Sanford was founded in 1927 when the Chicago, Rock Island and Gulf Railway extended its Amarillo–Liberal, Kansas, line through the area. The town was named for rancher James M. Sanford, who donated the land. Sanford was soon populated with oil boomers and oil company employees; however, the town never received the notoriety of Borger. During its first year, the Acme Lumber Yard was built on one end of Main Street, and at the other end stood a two-story hotel. Moon Mullins established a café.

By 1942, when we got there, many of the oil boomers had moved on, and Sanford had five businesses and a population of sixty. The hotel was still there, but the lumberyard and café were gone. We did have three carbon black plants, along with two gasoline refineries that were owned by Phillips Petroleum. We also had two grocery stores, a drugstore, and two Phillips gasoline stations.

Phillips Petroleum, at that time, was the largest producer of natural gas liquids in the United States, and the company built its first petroleum refinery in the Texas Panhandle. Everything was Phillips gasoline in those days. I used to say that I was 25 years old before I knew there was anything other than buffalo grass, mesquite trees, Phillips gasoline, barbed wire, and Bob Wills.

After Moon Mullins closed his café, he opened one of the grocery stores in town. Daddy butchered a beef and three hogs for him every Saturday morning. After I got a little older, he let me shoot them, and I still have that rifle, a little .22 short, lever-action Savage.

Daddy was working in one of the carbon black plants, and Mother was teaching school. I don't remember what Daddy's salary was, but Mother was making $1,100 a year.

Carbon black could be made as a by-product of natural gas. It was used primarily in the manufacture of rubber tires, but also as a coloring pigment in paints and dyes. The work was dirty and dangerous, but it paid better than a lot of other jobs.

Everybody in town had the same kind of job. The richest man in town was a night foreman at one of the carbon black plants. He made 25 cents an hour more than anybody else. And I guess we were poor, but I didn't know it. We were in the same class as everyone else in town. We were all in the same financial situation.

My sister Sue Anne was born in 1944. After three boys, Mother finally got a girl. As I look back now, I think having a girl is the only thing that saved Mother's sanity because us three boys dealt her a lot of misery, just doing things boys do. But Sue Anne stabilized things. (Two more boys would come along later, making us a family of eight.)

In late 1948, Daddy was working for Texoma Natural Gas Company and was transferred to a small compressor plant at Kingsmill, Texas, which is halfway between White Deer and Pampa. Kingsmill is only thirty-eight miles from Sanford, but I went to the fifth grade in White Deer. Then, in the summer of 1949, Mother and Sue Anne went to Iowa to see Mother's younger sister, and while they were there, my brother David was born. The rest of us kids went to Forestburg that summer, and my grandmother and aunts took care of us until Mother, Sue Anne, and David got home. Then we moved back to Sanford.

Mother always kept in close contact with our relatives in Montague County. The Texas Silver Zephyr was a passenger train that ran from Amarillo to Fort

Worth, and I can remember riding it down to Bowie, Texas, lots of times. One of our relatives would pick us up in Bowie and take us back to Forestburg so we could see our grandmother and all our aunts and uncles. The Silver Zephyr was really fast; at least, it seemed that way to me. To get on it, we had to first catch a freight train that had one passenger car and ride it from Sanford to Amarillo. I remember it took longer to go the fifty miles from Sanford to Amarillo on that freight train than it did the 300 miles from Amarillo to Bowie on the Silver Zephyr.

One of my earliest memories is of a trip Mother, Carroll, Barry, and I took down there. When we got ready to go home, Aunt Roxie, Daddy's sister, took us to Bowie to catch the train. We loaded up and got our seats in the first car. About the time the train started rolling, Mother realized she had Aunt Roxie's car keys in her purse. When the train stopped in Electra, Mother got off to send those keys back to Bowie. The train started rolling before Mother got back on, and I was scared to death. I must have been 5 years old; Carroll was 4, and Barry was a baby in my arms. All I could think of was, "How am I going to raise these boys by myself?" As the train picked up speed, I'm certain that the three of us made a tremendous amount of unpleasant noise, but then Mother showed up. She had caught the last car and walked all the way through the train to get to where we were.

I assume my wanting to be a cowboy started after we first moved to Sanford. The Sanford Ranch surrounded the town, which was built kinda like a banjo. A barbed wire fence circled it, and the only road there at that time came in from the south. The ranch cowboys would come from headquarters over in Carson County and work the cattle in that river country. Ranches didn't haul their horses in those days, like they do now, and the cowboys would ride right through town. I would stand on the side of the gravel street that ran in front of our house and watch them as they rode by, and I would be so jealous that I couldn't get on one of those horses and go with them.

But I had an idyllic childhood. Because Sanford was so rural, you didn't have to go very far to be in the wilderness, and I loved it. We were about half a mile south of the Canadian River, which ran all the way across the Panhandle. People had been living on that river for thousands of years, and there is so much history there. Just a handful of miles upstream from where I lived is one of the largest deposits of flint rock there is anywhere, and for the past 13,000 years, natives had shaped that flint into arrowheads, spear points, hide scrapers, and all kinds of other tools. It's called Alibates flint, and it was so prized by prehistoric hunters that many traveled more than a thousand miles to obtain it. Those who couldn't travel that far traded for it. Projectile points and other tools made of Alibates stone have been found as far north as Montana, as far south as Central Mexico, and east to at least the Mississippi River.

The last ones to use the flint were the Comanches, who made weapons and tools from it until as recently as the mid-1800s, when they were able to procure metal from the white man.

I spent every minute I could on that river bottom, and I found all kinds of artifacts. I learned how to spot an old spring where Indians had camped, and I learned how to find little piles of flint chips, where they had made their arrowheads and their tools.

I loved all of that. I loved the outdoors. I didn't know there was anything in the world other than nature and being outside. I couldn't stand to be indoors, and Mother didn't worry about my being outside for hours at a time.

I would sit out there on the big rocks on that riverbank, all by myself, and just look out across that vast country. And I would envision Indian tepees down there in that river bottom. One day I would be riding north with Charles Goodnight, who co-founded the famous Goodnight–Loving cattle trail, and the next day I would be fighting the white eyes with Comanche chief Quanah Parker.

The first book I read all the way through was *The No-Gun Man of Texas*, written by Laura V. Hamner, who devoted much of her life to recording and sharing the history of the Texas Panhandle. The book was about Charles Goodnight, whom Miss Hamner knew. I was hooked. From then on, the idea of cowboys and Indians was firmly ingrained in everything I wanted to do.

They used to call kids with big imaginations like that daydreamers, and they didn't want them to daydream. They wanted them to be realistic. Well, to me, that was realistic. I believe that a lot of the things I write about today were etched in my imagination during my childhood in the vast, rugged Texas Panhandle.

In the spring of 1944, when I was 5 years old, Daddy joined the Navy. Our country was fully engaged in the war by then, of course, and just about all the able-bodied men were going off to fight. He was assigned to an amphibious assault ship in the Asiatic-Pacific campaign and participated in the Battle of Iwo Jima. In the almost two years that he was gone, it was just Mother and us kids getting by at home.

My mother was a strong and resilient lady. She taught first grade, and she started off with me. When I was 5, I could read and write because I would watch her grade papers and she helped me learn to read the schoolbooks. By the time I got to first grade, I had memorized all the books that the class used, so I would finish my work and when she left the room to get a drink of water or use the restroom, I would help the kids who were struggling. I got a whipping almost every day for helping those kids, and then I got another at home that evening because she had to give me a whipping in school.

But I wouldn't take anything in the world for it. The most important thing she taught all of her kids was the ability to speak and spell properly. It was so important to her. Nearly every time we would start to complain about something, she would say, "There will come a time you will thank me for that," and I have, a zillion times.

She treated all of us the same. Every time one of us had a birthday, we all got a present. The one whose birthday it was got a bigger present than the rest of the kids, but everyone got a present. Every one of us knows she had a favorite, and each one of us thinks we're it.

She was a great psychologist. When I was 14, Dewayne Thomas lived across the street from us. His father was the richest man in town because he was the night foreman at the carbon black plant, and Dewayne was the only kid in town who had a car. It was a 1941 Ford coupe, and I still think that's the prettiest car ever made. One day, Dewayne wanted me to go with him to Fritch, which was seven miles away, to get a Coke, and Mother didn't want me to go. I was begging her, "Dewayne can't go by himself, I've got to go with him."

She looked at me and said, "I've taught you all I know about the difference between right and wrong. From this day forward, I will never tell you no. I will only tell you that I don't want you to do it if I disagree with your decision."

I didn't go to Fritch that day, and even today, as old as I am, when I start to make a decision, I think, "What would Mother think about that?" That's how powerful she was, and every one of us kids absolutely idolized her. She was truly our teacher.

Daddy was discharged from the Navy in December 1945. The war was over, and he came back to Sanford. Mother had bought us a house by that time; she paid $900 for it.

It wasn't all that much of a house: it was three oil drilling rig dog houses that someone had put together and made into one building. What the oil field called a dog house was a little wooden shack on the drill floor. It was used as a combination toolshed, lunchroom, and general meeting place for the driller and his crew. The dog houses were made of 1-by-12 lumber, with 1-by-4 planks nailed over the cracks between the 1-by-12s. They called it board-and-batten, or box-and-strip, and it wasn't all that uncommon. There were lots of early day ranch houses constructed that way.

We had a little living room, two bedrooms, and a kitchen. The only electricity in the whole house was a single line coming down in the middle of the kitchen ceiling; that was our only artificial light. Our heat was generated by natural gas. There was lots of natural gas in the Panhandle, so it was available and inexpensive. We had a Servel natural gas refrigerator. In 1990, a recall was issued, and the government warned consumers to stop using Servel gas refrigerators that had been manufactured between 1933 and 1957 because of the danger of carbon monoxide leakage. We never had any problems, but it might have been because our house was so drafty. There was plenty of circulation.

There was no insulation in the walls of the house, just tar paper on the inside. We did the same thing a lot of people did and glued newspapers onto that tar paper to create another layer. When the wind blew, you could see those newspapers fluttering.

If it was cold, we slept under quilts. Grandmother made blankets and quilts constantly. Some nights I might have had four or five quilts on top of me. There were three of us boys at the time, and we all slept in the same room. I had to sleep on the north side because I was the oldest. In the winter, I might wake up in the morning to find little rivulets of snow across my quilts. If we had a sandstorm, there would be little rivulets of sand that had sifted through the cracks in the wall. And during the drought in the '50s, there were plenty of sandstorms.

The house was sitting on piles of rocks, and the cracks in the floor were just as wide as the ones in the wall. We didn't have any carpet, and not very many rugs, so all we had on the floor was linoleum, and it got really cold.

We slept with our socks on, and at night, when we undressed, we would put our britches underneath the covers. Each morning, we would swing our feet off the side of the bed and put our boots on so we didn't have to step on that cold linoleum floor, and then we would pull our britches on. People used to kid me because I put my boots on first, and then my pants. Well, there was a reason for that, and I've done it all my life.

One time I was doing a show at Rough Creek Lodge near Glen Rose, Texas, for a group of people who were there for a meeting. This great big guy with a big, red face asked me, "Where'd you say you were from?"

I told him, "Sanford."

He said, "I'm from Skellytown," and then he added, "I've got to know something. Do you put your boots on before you put your britches on?"

I told him I did, and he turned to his wife.

"Margaret, come here. I want you to meet this boy. He's from Sanford."

She said, "Don't tell me you put your boots on before you put your pants on."

It was a very common thing. Skellytown is just twenty-six miles southeast of Sanford, and everyone in that area grew up the same way. Nobody wanted to step on that old, cold linoleum floor first thing in the morning.

The only bathroom we had was an outdoor toilet behind the house. We had running water in the kitchen, but we didn't have a hot water heater. We all bathed in a number 3 washtub, and Mother heated the water on a big old cast iron stove in the kitchen. Since I was the oldest, I had to bathe last—in the same water the other boys had already bathed in. When my sister Sue Anne came along, I had to empty that dirty water and then fill the tub up again for her so she would have fresh water.

We didn't think anything about it. Everybody we knew lived that way.

Even back then, I had already developed a taste for country music. Daddy played guitar pretty well, and he taught me to sing cowboy songs and Jimmie Rodgers songs, and I loved to listen to the Grand Ole Opry. On Saturday night, Mother would put a plug-in receptacle in the light socket so I could listen to the radio. I would sit there in a cane-bottom chair in the kitchen, in the dark, and listen to the Grand Ole Opry. You could either listen to the radio or have the light on, but you couldn't have both. During the day, when she didn't need the light, Mother would have the radio on. When it got dark, she would unplug the radio and screw in a light bulb.

One time Daddy came home with a light socket that had two plug outlets in it. You could have a bulb screwed in and plug something in on the side of it. I thought that was the greatest invention in the world. I didn't have to sit in the dark to listen to the Grand Ole Opry.

Many a night I would sit in that cane-bottom chair and dream of being on that stage, never knowing that one day I would stand in front of that microphone. When I finally got there, and the people I had been listening to since I was a little kid were all around me, I was so nervous I could hardly sing at all. Charlie Walker introduced me, and I remembered hearing Charlie Walker when I was a little kid sitting in that old kitchen. It was quite an experience.

Of course, we didn't have air conditioning in that old house, and in the summer, even though we lived nearly as far north as you could go in the state of Texas, it still got hot. In that old wooden house without any insulation, there was no way to keep the heat out. But when we finally got electricity in some other rooms, and Mother got a little extra money, she bought some fans that she set on stands at the end of our beds. And we kept the windows open. One thing about the Texas Panhandle, there is nearly always a breeze.

That was our air conditioning. But we didn't think we were underprivileged. Everybody we knew lived that way.

Mother was supporting us at that time. She was able to teach in the elementary school in Sanford with only the two-year degree she had gotten before she and Daddy were married. But she knew she needed more education. One summer, when I was about 11, Grandmother Mitchell came to Sanford and stayed with us while Mother went to summer school at North Texas State Teachers College and finished her bachelor's degree. She was the smartest woman I've ever known.

CHAPTER 2

GROWING UP

As I got a little older, I trapped coyotes and bobcats all along the Canadian River, and my buddy Don Creacy and I had a little pack of coon dogs. I don't remember exactly how many we had, but they were all blacks and tans except one old redbone female. Redbone is what they called a coonhound with a solid dark red coat. She could find those 'coons. We never did kill any of them. We just chased them all night in that river bottom, treed them, and then let them go.

My friend Tuss Fisher had an old one-eyed greyhound, and sometimes we would get up early in the mornings and run coyotes out on the flats until it was time to catch the school bus.

We sure didn't have any money back then, but all I needed was 57 cents to buy a box of .22 long rifle hollow points so I could shoot jackrabbits to feed my coon dogs. The only way we had of making any money was picking up Coke bottles alongside the road and taking them back to the stores for the deposit. Fifty-seven cents a box for .22 shells was a lot of money when I was picking up Coke bottles at 5 cents apiece. I picked up a lot of Coke bottles.

Horses have always been a big part of my life, although I didn't own one until I moved to California. When I was a kid, 500 feet on both sides of the river was open range. And it was good grass when everything else was dry. There was subterranean moisture around that riverbed. People from some of the little towns around would have horses that they couldn't feed in the winter so they would turn them out on that river.

As a result, my friends and I had a big herd of wild horses at our disposal. Well, we thought they were wild, but they were just saddle horses that had been turned out. Every once in a while, we would get them cornered in a box canyon and rope one and try to ride him. Of course, they nearly killed all of us.

We didn't have any saddles in the beginning, but I remember the time we put money together and bought a used McClellan saddle for $7 out of an ad in a *Frontier Times* magazine. I don't have any idea what happened to that saddle, but we got to where we wouldn't ride it because it didn't take long before we were so sore, we couldn't walk. It really galled us.

I had to go to high school in Phillips, which was a town about twenty-five miles away, on the other side of Borger, because our high school had burned down. We had to ride a school bus through Borger all the way to Phillips because Borger became populated so fast, they couldn't handle any more students. Phillips was named for the Phillips Petroleum oil refinery that was built there. The kids in Phillips didn't like us. They called us the "bus people."

I had to ride the bus because Mother didn't have a car. But in my senior year, Gene Packebush got a car with a radio in it. We would skip study hall and go to the parking lot and listen to Cactus Smith on KDDD in Dumas. He played nothing but Western swing.

My experience with cars was very limited since Mother didn't get a car until after I graduated from high school. Anytime I needed to go somewhere out of town, I either hitchhiked or caught a ride with a neighbor. While I was a junior in high school, Gene Packebush, Marvin Neeley, and I chipped in and bought a wrecked Ford Model A from Lou Steen. Even though it had been smashed up, it was still in pretty good shape, and he wanted $15 for it.

It took us a while to get the $15, but we finally got it done, and we overhauled that Model A every Friday night, whether it needed it or not. We got our replacement parts from a wrecked car that we bought from Tuffy Tucker for $25.

We cut the top off and built a rumble seat in the back so four of us could ride in it, and we painted it baby blue. Then we painted a Confederate flag on each door. After that, we welded a one-inch pipe on the fenders and flew a Texas flag on one side and a Confederate flag on the other. Boy, we were really something.

Those were the days when we ran everything on drip gasoline. If you didn't grow up in the oil fields, you don't know what drip gasoline was, but it's a condensate that forms in natural gas transmission lines. It settles in the bottom of those big 36-inch lines into a pot. A valve was on the end of a line from the pot to the surface, and if you opened that valve, pressure in the line would blow out the liquid. We would collect it in 55-gallon drums and use it in our Model A.

Nearly everyone had a 30-gallon drum in the back of their car so they wouldn't have to buy gasoline if they were out on the road. Gas cost 11 cents a gallon then, and the drip was free. They didn't make it in the summer, only in the winter, and you had to keep it cool. Daddy had some 55-gallon drums buried in our yard, and my uncle Johnny had a whole bunch of barrels of drip down in the hole underneath his grease rack. Everybody had drip barrels either buried in their garden or in their garage underneath the ground.

Even though it was free, you were supposed to pay 4 cents a gallon tax to the government. Government men—we called them revenuers—would stop and check you occasionally, but most people didn't worry about it. However, when a car was burning drip, you could smell it for a long way. It was very low octane, so it wouldn't run well in all vehicles, but it worked good in that Model A.

Occasionally, we'd see a white Ford come across those ridges and that would be the revenuers coming, trying to catch us running those drips. But they couldn't travel on those ranch trails and down the middle of those creeks like we could in that Model A.

Then our friend Melvin Cole got a '49 Ford pickup. The door was gone off the passenger side where he had run into a cattle guard, but we built a platform on the back so it would hold two 55-gallon drums, and we welded a school bus seat up on top so we could sit up there and hunt. Then we took some old wheels and mounted them so they would fit exactly on a railroad track. The best drip was on the north side of the river because it had less phosphorus in it and didn't stink so bad. We would take that old pickup down to the railroad track, mount those wheels, straddle the track, and take off across that river bridge to get that good gas.

It was a mile from bank to bank across that river, and we would draw straws to see who was going to jump last if we met a train. We never did meet one, but we would sit up there on that school bus seat with a spotlight and a rifle, and we would hunt jackrabbits, coyotes, and bobcats while we were on the way to get that drip.

There were lots of weekends that we would take off on Saturday morning real early if we had a football game on Friday night, or Friday evening after school if we didn't, and we would go up or down the river and hunt arrowheads and fossils all day and all night. We would get back home on Sunday evening.

That's how I grew up.

CHAPTER 3

POLIO

The summer before my junior year in high school, my father moved to Borger.

I loved Daddy dearly. I admired him and I tried to copy things he did. He was a master stonemason; he could finish concrete like you couldn't imagine. He had a very analytical mind, and he could build anything. He could walk into a manufacturing plant yard and in three or four days tell you how everything worked. But he had a demon. He didn't know how to accept responsibility, and he hid this shortcoming with alcohol. He kept losing his job because he would get so confident that he knew everything. He thought he could do the job better than anyone else, the boss would disagree with him, and he'd get fired. It was pretty tough on Mother, and in August 1954, she divorced him just a month before my brother Danny was born.

I loved playing football, and that fall I was going to start at left end for the Phillips High School Blackhawks. We had a good team, and we knew it. Our coach was Harold "Chesty" Walker, and there was a time in the 1950s that he was known as the winningest coach in Texas. While he was at Phillips, he coached eighteen district champions and one state champion team.

Coach Walker's best friend was Coach Tom Tipps, who was an assistant coach to Bear Bryant at Texas A&M, and Coach Tipps had told me that when I graduated, he wanted me to come play football at A&M. That fit right into my plans, because my goal was to become a veterinarian. Texas A&M had the only veterinary school in Texas, and the only way I could afford to go to school there was with a football scholarship.

I had spent that summer of 1954 working on my uncle's farm in Iowa, and I got home the night before two-a-days started the next morning. In high school football, just before the season started, players would practice two times a day, morning and afternoon. That two-week stretch was called two-a-days.

I woke up before daylight the morning of the first game, and my head was killing me. The pain was so bad that I remember lying in that bed just screaming. Mother walked down the street two blocks to where the school superintendent lived. His wife had had polio, and Mother got her to come look at me. She told Mother, "Yes, he has polio. Let's get him to the hospital."

Since Mother didn't have a car, they took me in their car to the hospital. The doctor there kept telling me, "You'll get over this. You'll get the feeling back in your arm." But he didn't know, because I was the first polio victim he had ever seen.

Polio is a highly contagious virus that can cause nerve injury leading to paralysis, difficulty breathing, and sometimes death. In the 1950s, parents were literally terrified because children were coming down with the disease and no one knew where it came from, how their children contracted it, or what to do about it. In some cities, swimming pools and movie theaters were closed on the chance that the polio virus might be in the water or in the air. And even if those places weren't closed, many parents forbid their children to go to them. No one knew what to do.

I was 15 years old when I was diagnosed with polio, and I was scared to death. My best friend when I was 11 was Erwin Henderson. He got bulbar polio, which is one of the variations of the disease, and he died. Other than the superintendent's wife, he was the only person I had known who had it, and I wondered if I was about to die.

In my case, the disease cost me the use of my left shoulder and arm. That included my hand and my fingers. I couldn't do anything with them.

I went to the hospital with polio on September 6, 1954. And if my mother didn't already have enough to worry about, four days later my brother Danny was born by cesarean. Mother would hold him up to the window at the hospital so I could see him from the yard out front. At that time, we didn't know how contagious polio was, so everyone was scared and very cautious. It was about three months before I got to hold Danny.

Sanford was a close-knit community, and when I came down with polio, the men in town built me a bedroom on the back of that old junkie house, and they built us a bathroom. When mother got home from the hospital with Danny, we had a shower and an indoor toilet. That was a godsend for her, too.

Once my fever went away, they let me out of the hospital and let me go back to school. But the first day I was back I thought, "You know, if I'm going to get ready for that next ball game, I had better get in shape." I didn't even think about not being able to move my left arm. I just figured I was weak and that my strength would come back with exercise. I suited up, ran about ten yards, and passed out. I was out for two hours; it's a wonder it didn't kill me.

For the next two weeks after that, Coach Jackson and Coach Williams got me out of study hall every day and put me in a whirlpool for an hour. I think that's the only thing that saved my life, because I probably would have been bent double if they hadn't done that. I have no spinal problems, like so many other polio victims do.

Then the doctor sent me down to Plainview, Texas, about seventy miles south of Amarillo, to a hospital that was known nationwide for treating polio patients. They didn't have a room for me, so they put me on a gurney and rolled me into the iron lung ward.

Polio patients whose respiratory system had been affected by polio to the extent they couldn't breathe were placed in what was called an iron lung. An iron lung is a mechanical respirator that encloses most of a person's body and, to stimulate breathing, it varies the air pressure in the enclosed space. It just helps someone breathe when they are unable to do it on their own.

There were fourteen kids from all over the United States in iron lungs in that ward. I had to lie there and listen to those iron lungs pump air 24 hours a day, sucking air in and blowing air out, and even though I had a crippled shoulder and arm, I wasn't nearly as bad off as those kids. It was at that point that I made a covenant with the Lord. I said, "God, if you'll get me out of here, you'll never hear me complain about having polio or the fact that I only have one good arm." He got me out of there, and I've lived up to that pledge.

But those iron lungs had a horrible sound as they compressed the chest and made the person breathe. At Fort Concho in San Angelo, in the old hospital, there's an old iron lung. I was there some years ago, and when I walked around the corner and saw that thing, I nearly collapsed. It brought back all those memories.

Alex Cord, the actor, was a good friend of mine, and he was a victim of polio. Alex died in 2021 at the age of 89, but as a youth he spent a long time in an iron lung. The disease compromised his lungs, but it didn't keep him from doing what he wanted to do. He was a real inspiration to me, and I didn't meet him until we were both grown men.

I also have some friends who were unable to get over what polio did to them. They lost the use of their legs, or their arms, and spent the rest of their lives in wheelchairs. They never got over it. They would sit around and say, "Poor me, why did this happen to me?" My attitude was, "This happened to me and I'm not going to let it conquer me." By embracing that attitude, I found that you can take almost any situation that is negative, lose the negativity, find something positive, and go on with life. It's been a great lesson.

I've never regretted having polio. It made me learn to adapt because I'm not like everybody else. Mother gave me a poem by Edgar A. Guest called "It Couldn't Be Done," and I've never forgotten it. The main verse I remember says,

Somebody said that it couldn't be done,
But he with a chuckle replied
That "maybe it couldn't," but he would be one
Who wouldn't say so till he'd tried.
So he buckled right in with a bit of a grin,
On his face. If he worried he hid it.
He started to sing as he tackled the thing
That couldn't be done, and he did it.

Sometime in 1954, Dr. Jonas Salk developed a vaccine that prevented polio. The vaccine was rolled out in January 1955 and nearly everyone in our country lined up to be vaccinated, either by injection or by eating a sugar cube that contained the vaccine. Dr. Salk's vaccine eliminated polio in nearly all the developed countries of the world, although there are still some occurrences in Asia and Africa. In the United States, the last case of naturally occurring polio was in 1979.

Because the disease was eliminated in the US in 1994, many people today have never heard of it. Within the last couple of years, I was going to a physical therapist who was in her twenties. When she saw my crippled arm, she asked, "What happened to your arm? Did a bull get you down?"

I said, "No, I had polio."

She asked, "What's polio?"

I thought, how great it is that a 20-year-old person who is in the medical profession has never heard of polio. Dr. Salk coming up with that vaccine was a wonderful thing.

I had a paper route before I had polio, and from the money I earned delivering those papers, I was able to buy a new green 26-inch Western Flyer bicycle. Up to that point, all my bicycles had been put together with parts from a local dump and trades I made with my friends. I was proud of that bicycle, but when I was probably 12 or 13 years old, I left it out in front of the yard one day. Daddy accidentally ran over it. I was devastated.

Lou Steen was custodian at the school and was Mother's best friend. He came by our house every day after he cleaned the school and had coffee with Mother. Lou had come to the area before Sanford was a town. He had been a government trapper, and I just loved him. He would tell me stories about trapping wolves, and he was kind of a childhood hero to me because I could just see myself trapping those wolves and being out for weeks on end, living in the wild.

I was sitting on the porch, bawling my eyes out that day when he came by. He asked me what was wrong, and I told him about my bicycle.

He said, "Well, let me tell you something. Things that happen to you today that are good are to make life pleasant today. Things that happen to you that are bad are to toughen you up for tomorrow."

I kept that in my mind while I was recuperating from polio. When I was learning to live without the use of my left shoulder, that story kept coming back to me. I told myself, "There's going to be more of this, so accept it, turn it around, make it positive, and do the best you can with it so that you'll have a better idea how to deal with it the next time it comes around."

When I got home from Plainview, Coach Walker said, "Even though you can't play football, I'll make you our manager so you can travel with the team." I did that, and we won state that year. And even though I wasn't playing, I was there with the team.

I was also on the track team. I got a saddle maker to build a sling for my arm so I could run the half mile. I don't remember doing very well; I know I didn't go to state. But before I got polio, I had been pole vaulting, and I was up to 11 feet. I planned to set the state record, but of course I didn't.

I tried not to let polio ruin the last two years I had in high school, but Mother knew that I needed help. She called Mrs. Harry Miller, a piano teacher who lived about two and a half miles from town. Mrs. Miller had a mandolin, and she sold it to us for $10. Mother paid it off a dollar a month.

I rode my bicycle over to Mrs. Miller's to take lessons. In the beginning, the fingers on my left hand were just like pieces of spaghetti; I had no control over them whatsoever. She showed me how to hold that mandolin and concentrate on one finger at a time until I got that finger strong enough to keep from muting the strings against the neck. Then we worked until I could make a two-finger chord, and then I made a three-finger chord. That mandolin saved my life.

I kept my paper route, and I was making $6 a month. Probably about the middle of my senior year in high school, when I got some strength in my fingers, Mother and I together bought a Guild guitar, and paid $129 for it. Every month, I chipped in $3 and she chipped in $3, and we paid it out. I still have both of those instruments today. I loaned the mandolin to the museum in Spearfish, South Dakota, but it's still mine, and I have the guitar at my house. I played it until I had been out of college two years and bought another one.

I can only play open chords on a guitar. That means that I hang my left thumb on the top of the neck and play chords that originate in the first two or three frets on the guitar neck. Since I can't move my arm, I can't play bar chords or move my hand up and down the neck of the guitar. But I've made it work. I've written lots of songs that way.

Golf helped me get over polio, too. I don't mean it healed me or anything like that, but it helped get me through the trauma of it. We had a little nine-hole golf course at Sanford. It was across the road from the Phillips gasoline plant and the men who worked at the plant had built it. They kept part of the pasture on the Sanford Ranch mowed short for the fairways, and they built greens out of oiled sand. When you hit a ball up on that sand, you had to rake an alley so you could putt it to the hole. We thought that was big time.

One day, when I was in the sixth grade, I was fooling around down in the Sanford junkyard, and I found a rusted old putter head and a seven-iron head. Two friends and I whittled down old broom handles, put the heads on them, and the three of us played golf with those two clubs.

We didn't have any money to buy golf balls, but at the end of the first fairway was a sump pond from the gasoline plant, and there were a lot of balls in there. It was oily and gunky, but we would get in there in our shorts, wade around, and feel those balls with our toes. You can't believe how filthy we were, but when we came out, we had a handful of golf balls. Some of them hadn't been in there long and they were still good. The golfers who had hit them in there would pay us a dime to get their good balls back. But the rest of the balls sometimes squished when you hit them, and sometimes it was like hitting a rock because they had been in there for years. But that's how we learned to play golf.

About the time I got into high school, one of the men who worked at the plant put a set of old clubs together for us. The three of us would share that set of golf clubs and walk around those nine holes every chance we got. We even dyed some of those golf balls pink and green so we could play in the snow. We were really into it.

The guitar and golf saved my hand. When I got older and could buy a set of clubs and was able to play on golf courses with grass greens, I thought I had died and gone to Heaven.

CHAPTER 4

COLLEGE

When I couldn't play football, I lost my scholarship to Texas A&M. But Coach Tipps knew that I wanted to be a veterinarian, so he said, "I'm going to set you up with Smokey Harper, who's our trainer. You can work for Smokey, learn to be a trainer, and travel with the team just as if you were a player."

The summer after I graduated from high school, I started looking for a job. Without a scholarship, I was going to have to pay my way through college. I had been promised a job as a trainer for the football team, but I needed money to start the semester. So, Jerry Tatum and I decided we would go on wheat harvest.

Every spring, when the wheat starts ripening in South Texas, crews with trucks and combines harvest wheat for the farmers who do not have trucks and combines. They usually work the same farms every season, saving the farmers the cost of investing in harvesting equipment. As the harvest crews finish an area, they just keep moving north through those areas where the wheat ripens a little later in the year, up through the Texas Panhandle, Kansas, and the other states, all the way to the Canadian border. Harvest crews often hire young men to drive both trucks and combines. Jerry and I knew that, and because I had spent five summers working on my uncle's farm in Iowa, I knew how to drive a combine. So we drove up to Gruver, a town about fifty miles north of Sanford, where there was a lot of wheat grown. We were going to get us a job with one of the harvest crews. We were too late; they had already finished the Texas Panhandle and were up in Kansas.

But we got a job unloading grain railroad cars at the elevator, using what they called a moldboard, which was a big piece of heavy plywood with handles. Through a series of pulleys, it operated similarly to a Fresno scraper that was used to build ditches and dirt stock tanks. We unloaded ten cars, but that didn't last all summer, and I had to have another job.

That was the summer they built the cloverleaf in Borger, which was an overpass where Highway 152 crossed Highway 207. I got a job helping the powder monkey, who was the man who used explosives to blast the rocks out of an area where they were going to build a highway. He showed me how to drill the holes, set the powder, set the timer, make sure everyone was out of range, and hit the plunger. On my second day, he quit, and Pete Gilvin, the contractor, made me the powder monkey.

By the end of summer, I had saved $595. I rode down to College Station with Jimmy Gray and Norman Kendrick, two boys I had played football with and who had gotten scholarships to play at A&M. I registered for enrollment, and it took every dime of that $595 to check me into the dorm and pay for tuition, fees, and books for the first semester. After I finished all that, I went over to see Smokey Harper.

I said, "Mr. Harper, I'm here. I've checked into the dorm, but it's not the athletic dorm."

He told me, "No, you probably wouldn't stay in the athletic dorm." Then he said, "Let's go in and I'll introduce you to coach Bryant."

I didn't know who Bear Bryant was. I hadn't listened to the football games on the radio and I didn't read the newspaper. But I spent about thirty minutes in his office, and he was very kind to me. He said, "I'm so glad you're going to be with us. You'll travel with the team. Mr. Harper will show you what to do and when to do it, and you're going to have a good time."

So, we went back into Smokey's office and I asked, "Mr. Harper, what does this job pay?"

He said, "Son, this job doesn't pay anything, but if you stay with us for three years, and if you get to be good enough to make an assistant trainer, then we'll give you a full ride and a Chevrolet car for your senior year."

I said, "I can't stay. I've already spent all my money; I don't have any way to stay alive."

Smokey tried to get me a job in the student center, but it only paid $12 a week, and that wasn't going to be enough. So, I called my Aunt Roxie in Forestburg, and she sent me $35 to pay for a bus ticket home.

I got my money back from Texas A&M and I enrolled in Frank Phillips College, which was a junior college in Borger, and finished out the year. That way I could live at home and go to college.

Mother had us attend church regularly, and I always headed to the front pew when the doors opened at the church. I was intrigued with what the preacher had to say. I made every Sunday school meeting, and any time the youth people at the Methodist church went anywhere, I wanted to be on board because I loved it.

While I was in college at Frank Phillips, I started going to church in Borger. I would hitchhike over there on Sunday mornings, and Reverend Newton Starnes became one of my real heroes in life. Everything about Newton Starnes was positive, and he taught me how to overcome a lot of my insecurities and worries and turn them to positive advantage. He decided that I needed to be a lay pastor.

All the preachers in North Texas would take a vacation in the summer and I would fill in a Sunday or two at some of the churches. I really got into it, and I decided maybe this is what I should do. Then one Sunday morning, I realized that what I liked about it was that those people were listening to me. I liked the show business part of it, and I realized that if I continued with this, the Lord wasn't going to like me. I decided not to be a preacher.

But I still wanted to be a veterinarian, and I knew that I needed to go to one of the larger colleges to have any chance of getting admitted to veterinary school at Texas A&M. My English teacher at Frank Phillips told me about a state program that would provide funding for continuing education for victims of polio. Mother wrote the agency, and the people there told her I qualified to have my books, room, tuition, and any required fees paid. All I had to worry about was a meal ticket. I had heard that there was a good agriculture department at West Texas State College in Canyon, Texas, which was only about seventy miles away, so I decided to go there.

Mother had an old suitcase, and in it I packed six pairs of Levi's, three white shirts, and some underwear. I was wearing a pair of black Tony Lama boots with blue stitching in the tops, and I had put cardboard in the bottoms to cover up the holes in the soles. I got out on the highway with that suitcase and my guitar and hitchhiked to Canyon.

When I got to the college, I went to the administration building and told them I wanted to enroll and I wanted to study agriculture. They set me up some classes and assigned me to a dorm, and I became a college student.

I had that scholarship, but I had to work to survive. I started racking balls at the pool hall in the evenings for $3.50 a week, Monday through Friday, and I shocked feed on Saturdays and Sundays.

Lots of people didn't like to shock feed because it was hard on your back. The farmers had binders that would cut the feed stalks and tie them into bundles on the ground. After the bundles dried, I would go down the row, pick those bundles up with a pitchfork, and stand a group of them against each other, kinda in a tepee fashion. That kept the feed from rotting on the ground. All of that bending over to pick up those bundles was tough, but that wasn't the only problem. Those of us who were shocking feed also had to watch for rattlesnakes and skunks under those bundles.

My junior and senior years, I taught freshman ag labs for 50 cents an hour, and I fed cows at the college dairy for 75 cents an hour. I also started a few 2-year-old colts for some local ranchers. They paid me $20 a day, which I thought was an enormous amount of money. I didn't have a saddle, so I could only work for people who had a saddle I could use. But I did anything I could to make some money.

Even while I was in college, I thought about the times I had spent in the Canadian River Valley, looking for arrowheads, and how much fun it was, so I took advantage of Palo Duro Canyon, which wasn't but about fifteen miles from where I was living.

Palo Duro Canyon is the second largest canyon in the United States, and it's just filled with history. Supposedly, the first non-Indian to see the canyon was Francisco Coronado, who came by in the 1500s on his search for the Seven Cities of Gold. He named it Palo Duro because of the numerous cedar trees in the canyon. *Palo duro* is Spanish for "hard wood."

Indians had spent winters in Palo Duro Canyon for hundreds of years. All kinds of game was available for food, the canyon walls gave them protection from the north winds, and the headwaters of the Red River, which runs through the canyon, provided plenty of water. Palo Duro Canyon is also the site of the last major Indian battle in Texas, where Colonel Ranald Mackenzie and the 4th US Cavalry defeated a large contingent of Plains Indians and ended what was called the Red River War. I loved that canyon, and there were lots of weekends that

I would get a friend, Joe Peterman, to take me there. Gasoline was 11 cents a gallon then, so I would give Joe a quarter to take me to the edge of the canyon on Friday afternoon and then pick me up on Sunday afternoon.

I paid $1 for a mummy sleeping bag, 50 cents for a backpack, and 25 cents for a knapsack, and I would pack saltine crackers, summer sausage, cheddar cheese, and a canteen full of fresh water. When Joe dropped me off, I would follow an old Indian trail down to the bottom of that canyon and spend the weekend down there all by myself, hunting arrowheads and fossils. It was exactly what I did in the Canadian River Valley as I was growing up, and I still enjoyed it.

This also was the time when I really started writing songs with my guitar, and that gave me the opportunity to become friends with some great musicians. One of them was Don Lanier, who was from Sanford. He and I were friends there, but when we finished junior high, Donnie didn't continue on to Phillips High School with the rest of us. His father was transferred to a plant on the north side of the river, close to Dumas, so he went to high school at Dumas. Jimmy Bowen also went to high school at Dumas and, following graduation, both of them went to West Texas State, where they became friends with a boy from Canyon named Buddy Knox. In 1955, those three formed a band called Buddy Knox and the Rhythm Orchids. They had a number one record and several in the top 20. Buddy played guitar and sang, Jimmy played bass, and Donnie played lead guitar.

They recorded at the Norman Petty Studio in Clovis, New Mexico, which is where Buddy Holly and the Crickets, Jimmie Dale Gilmore, Jimmy Gilmer, the Fireballs, Roy Orbison, and a bunch of others first recorded. Norman charged $150 for 24 hours of studio time. You could stay there all night long and record, and then Norman would take those recordings to New York and try to get record contracts.

For seventeen straight years, at least one million-selling record a year came out of that studio. Today, the Norman Petty Studio is a city museum in Clovis.

Buddy Knox had a brand new '59 Ford hardtop convertible. I thought that was the most unbelievable car I'd ever seen in my life. They would come home from one of their tours and we would ride around in it. We would take our guitars and stand on the grass outside the girls' dorm and play songs.

But they were gone on tour a lot, so I fell in with some other guys who played music. I put a little band together, and we played at the VFW Hall for $5 most Saturday nights. I called the band Russell Don and the Premiers. There were five of us. We got a dollar apiece per show, and we thought we were stealing them blind.

I had a flat-top haircut and wore black horn-rimmed glasses. John Mason, from Matador, Texas, played piano for our little group. He wore black trousers stuck in his boot tops and a white shirt with a red garter on his sleeve. He could beat the fool out of those ivories. He went on to become a great chemist and is now Dr. John Mason.

Little Joe Powers played banjo. He later became a cement contractor in Arlington, Texas. Joe Nolan played guitar, and Asa Atchley played bass. After he graduated from college, Asa became the Canyon police chief.

One day a man from Miami, Texas, called and said he wanted us to perform at the Miami National Cow Calling Contest, which is a festival the town holds every year as a part of the Old Settlers' Reunion. He said he had $150 to pay us. Miami is a small town right at the top of the Texas Panhandle. We played that Cow Calling Contest, had the best time, and thought we were rich.

Ray Winkler, who ran KZIP Radio in Amarillo, had some shows at the Civic Center occasionally, and he would let us open for those shows. One time we opened for Johnny Horton, and another time we were on the same billing with Justin Tubb, Ernest Tubb's oldest son, who was the headliner of the show. My little band and I were in second position, and in third was an unknown singer by the name of Johnny Cash. The last person in the lineup was a guy named Elvis Presley. The crowd booed Elvis offstage. They didn't like what he was doing at all. But he came back six weeks later and sold out that auditorium for six shows in one day. His rise to stardom was meteoric. I jokingly like to say that Elvis opened for me in the early days.

Ray had us open for two Jim Reeves concerts, and Jim and I became buddies. He's one of the men who is most responsible for what I do today. He would let me send him tapes of songs I had written, and every time I sent him one, he would write me back. He would say, "Red, they're not quite right, not what I'm looking for, but keep trying." Jim gave me the incentive to write a better song.

My little band and I went to Clovis and recorded some songs that I had written, although I have no idea how we put $150 together in one wad. Norman took the master to New York with some other recordings. The rest of them got recording contracts with record labels, but we struck out. I didn't try recording again until I had been in Hollywood for three years.

I had a couple of cowboy friends at college, Buck Ramsey and Barton Riley, and they wanted me to be a bull rider. They thought it would be something for me, a one-armed man, to ride a bull. They built a bucking barrel on campus by Conner Hall, and we would go down there every night and ride it. A bucking barrel is a 55-gallon drum suspended in the air by four ropes coming off the edges, front and back. It was made to buck by people pulling on those ropes. They would try to buck me off that barrel, but I learned to ride it really well.

About this time, the intramural rodeo was coming up, and Walt Alsbaugh was the stock contractor. He had a big, gray Brahman bull they called Number One. I drew him, rode him to the buzzer, and I won the bull riding. I thought I was a bull rider from then on.

Of course, I held onto the bull rope with my right hand, and since I couldn't hold my other arm in the air, away from the bull, I had to tie it against my body with an elastic bandage. If I hadn't, it would have just flopped around. If it had touched the bull during the ride, I would have been disqualified. I rode bulls in amateur rodeos for about three years. I never did get bucked off, but other than in that first intramural rodeo, I never won a dime.

One Fourth of July, my brother Carroll and a couple of other guys were headed to Red River, New Mexico, so I went with them. On the way, we stopped at the rodeo in Clayton, New Mexico, and I drew the same bull that I had ridden in the intramural rodeo. About two jumps into the arena, the bull turned back to the right and the spur leather on my left foot broke. I lost my balance, because without a free arm to help keep my balance, my spurs were all I had. I flew off that bull's back like I had been shot from a cannon, and I hit the chute gate. I cracked some ribs, and I got up hurting so badly I could hardly stand it. I knew right then that if I ever broke my bad arm, it might never heal, and I just didn't want to take that chance. I walked out into the arena and picked up my bull rope, found the spur that I'd lost, took my other spur off, and gave them both to Carroll. I told him, "You ride the bulls from now on. I'm going to play dances."

After I had been in college a couple of years, Dr. M. R. Calliham, who was head of the Agriculture Department, told me, "I know you want to go to vet school. I'm going to Texas A&M this next semester and I'll be department head of the large animal clinic. If you will do a good job here and complete all your pre-vet requirements, I'll get you into vet school at Texas A&M."

So that was something to shoot for. But then I started thinking. I didn't want to work on cats and dogs, I wanted to work on horses and cows. And if I became a large animal veterinarian, with my arm the way it was, there was a good chance I would get somebody hurt, and maybe myself killed. When I was

Me and my brothers horseback, our favorite place to be. (L–R): Danny, David, Barry, Carroll (whom we lost in 2019), and me.

young and had two arms, I wasn't afraid of the devil himself. But when I lost the use of my left shoulder, I became more cautious, and I knew I couldn't do it.

Then Dr. Charles Smallwood took over the Agriculture Department, and right before I graduated, he told me, "I've got an offer for you." He knew I loved entomology, and he said, "I've got a teaching scholarship for you at Kansas State University where you can get your master's in entomology, and your doctorate, too, if you want to."

I turned down both offers, Texas A&M vet school and Kansas State. I was ready to finish school and go to work.

I graduated from West Texas State College in 1960 with a bachelor's degree in animal science and agronomy, and when I walked across that stage, Mother was right behind me. She got her master's degree that night.

Mother had six kids and taught school for forty-eight years. She loved her family more than anything in the world. She took care of us. I don't know how in the world she did it, but she fixed breakfast for us every morning. Every evening, she washed clothes and fixed supper.

When I was about to graduate from college, I still didn't have a car, and I didn't have any credit, so Mother co-signed a note for me to buy a 1956 Ford

Crown Victoria. It didn't matter what we needed; she was always there for us.

After graduation, I went to work for Fred Dines, who owned Western Grain and Supply in Amarillo. Fred was a distributor for all kinds of ag chemicals. At that time, there were millions of bushels of grain stored in elevators and barns across the panhandle. Insects were a real problem with grain storage, and I treated all the grain storage facilities with cyanide and bromide to kill the insects. I was making $1.25 an hour. My take-home pay was about $40 a week.

I got a promotion to salesman, and I traveled some, but then I found a better job with Shamrock Oil and Gas Corporation. Shamrock was putting in an anhydrous ammonia plant at Sunray, Texas, and needed someone with an agriculture degree to help sell the product. Anhydrous ammonia is a type of nitrogen fertilizer and is used a lot in the farming country of the upper Texas Panhandle.

But until they got their plant up and running, they put me in the gasoline division, and once again I hit the road. They assigned me a territory that included Colorado, Utah, Idaho, Wyoming, and Northern New Mexico. I had an apartment in Pueblo, Colorado, that I shared with my good friend Gary Johnson. Today, Gary's son Trent Johnson owns Greeley Hat Works in Greeley, Colorado. I didn't see that apartment much; I was on the road twenty-eight days a month. I would get back to Pueblo one weekend a month. I traveled all over the Intermountain West and was responsible for the advertising programs for 176 service stations.

I had a lot of wonderful experiences on the road with Shamrock Oil and met a lot of people who are still friends to this day. I got a tremendous education sitting on the street corner with a clicker so I could report back to the home office in Amarillo how many cars went by a certain intersection in a day. They used that count to judge where they were going to build the next station. Once they made a decision, they would buy the property and send the contractor out to build the station. I was the construction supervisor for the company, and when the station was complete, I would hire the crew, teach them how to clean windshields and check the batteries and the belts, and see if there was anything else we could sell the customers besides gasoline. Once they got the anhydrous ammonia plant set up, I moved back to Amarillo and started setting up distributorships for that product.

While I was on the road, the hootenanny craze had spread all over the country. There were folk singers everywhere. I knew where I was going to be two months in advance, because my schedule was laid out for me at the home office in Amarillo. I had bought a new guitar by then, a Gibson SJ-200 that I had gotten from a friend who needed some money. I paid $150 for it, and those guitars today sell for around $5,000.

I would book into the coffeehouses in the towns where I was scheduled to be, and I would take that guitar, sit on a stool, and sing cowboy songs. They paid me $25 a night, plus all the beer I could drink, every Friday and Saturday night. I was making a hundred dollars a week for the oil company, and $50 a week playing cowboy songs and telling jokes. It was a good life; I just didn't see how it could be any better.

CHAPTER 5

HOLLYWOOD

Buddy Knox and the Rhythm Orchids became superstars with all their hits, but then Buddy got drafted into the army. That ended the Rhythm Orchids, so Jimmy Bowen moved to Hollywood and went to work for Frank Sinatra's Reprise Records as a producer. It wasn't long afterward that Donnie Lanier followed him out there and became well known as an in-studio guitar player. One night, Donnie called and said, "We need some help and we don't like to depend on people we don't know. What are you doing?"

I said, "Well, I'm still with Shamrock."

He asked me, "Why don't you come to California?"

I had just bought a brand spanking new 1964 Chevrolet Super Sport Impala convertible, maroon and silver. I quit my job as assistant sales manager of the ag division at Shamrock—I could have stayed there the rest of my life—and hooked a 5x7 U-Haul trailer, with everything I owned in the world in it, behind that Chevrolet convertible and I went to California.

The first day I was there I got a ticket for hauling my trailer in the wrong lane on the freeway. I didn't know it was against the law; it all looked wide open to me. The second day, I bumped somebody in front of me, so I had a little collision on the freeway. By then, if I had had a hundred dollars to rent that trailer to haul my stuff back to Amarillo, I'd have never stayed in California. I didn't have the money, so I had to stay, and thank goodness I did. It started an adventure that I still live with today because I learned so much about myself, about the music industry, and about people.

By this time Jimmy Bowen had married recording artist Keely Smith, and he lived over in Toluca Lake, which is an affluent Los Angeles neighborhood only about twelve miles from downtown. He had become the most important producer in the record business and was recording Dean Martin and Frank Sinatra, among others. He was eventually responsible for getting Lee Hazlewood, who was a songwriter and record producer, to record Nancy Sinatra, and he signed First Edition and many more. He cut lots and lots of records.

Every producer had to have a union contractor, and Donnie Lanier was Jimmy's union contractor. Donnie hired the musicians Jimmy needed for the records he was producing, and he had to make sure the recording sessions didn't go over three hours. If you went three hours and 30 seconds, you had to pay the musicians time and a half for the session. If you went one minute over three hours, it was double time. Jimmy would have as many as forty musicians and twelve background singers for both Dean and Frank, so the union contractor was important.

Donnie was living by himself, so he and I rented a second-floor apartment in North Hollywood. I got a job selling industrial chemicals for Van Waters & Rogers, and my territory was Hollywood. I wasn't involved in the California music industry in the beginning, but I hung out with Jimmy and Donnie and the group that they were friends with, which included Roger Miller, Glen Campbell, and Lee Hazlewood. And there were some others, so I got to know a lot of people in the music business.

But my office was way over on the east side of Los Angeles. I was spending four hours a day on the freeway, cussing every minute of it. I got home one afternoon, and Donnie hadn't even been downstairs. He had been working the telephone all day, trying to hire musicians to record with Dean Martin and Frank Sinatra. I stopped and got the mail, and was looking at it as I walked in.

Donnie was sitting in his bedroom, on the edge of his bed, picking his guitar. I asked him, "Donnie, what are you doing?"

He said, "I have this little piece of melody bouncing around in my head that I can't do anything with," and he would pick some more. About that time, the phone rang, and he said, "Oh, hell, here we go again. Just let it ring." Then he looked up at me and grinned, played a couple of chords on his guitar, and sang, "Here we go again."

I immediately came back with, "She's back in town again," and Donnie sang, "I'll take her back again." I added, "One more time."

We sat down and finished the other verses in the song "Here We Go Again" in about ten minutes. I mean, it just poured out. I don't think we changed a single line.

Then, we called Jimmy. He and Keely were just sitting down to supper. Donnie said, "Jim, we wrote a hit."

Jimmy said, "Well, come on over and play it for me."

Toluca Lake was close to where we lived, so we drove over there that evening and played the song for Jimmy. He said, "Oh, I love that. Cut me a demo on it and I'll show it to Dean in the morning."

A Dean Martin record was way outside my wildest dreams, so we started making some calls. There was a little studio down on Ventura Boulevard where Three Dog Night and Steppenwolf recorded. I knew the guy who owned the studio and was the engineer. I called him that evening and he said, "Sure, there's nobody in the studio. Come on in."

We had to get a band together, so I called Jerry Allison, who played drums for Buddy Holly. I knew Jerry when we were back at West Texas State. I called Don Randi, who's a great jazz pianist even today, to play piano, and I got Larry Knechtel to play bass. Larry had a group called Bread. Donnie played rhythm guitar, and I got Glen Campbell to play lead guitar and sing. In twenty minutes, we cut the best record that's ever been cut on that song, and it's been recorded sixty-three times.

Then we went back to Jimmy's house with the record. He said, "I'll show it to Dean in the morning."

Dean listened to it and said, "You know, we're just coming off a country song and it didn't sell but a half million copies. Let's hang onto it and see what this other one does."

Jimmy said, "No, it's a hit song. The boys know it. I'm going to turn them loose."

A friend of mine named Ronnie Green was running a publishing company, Pamper Music, for Ray Price. The next day, I called Ronnie and he said, "Hey, Ray's in town. He's sitting out in front of my office in his bus right now."

I ran over there and played the song for Ray. He said, "Oh, I like that, Red. If you will let me have the publishing, I'll cut it."

"No, sir, there's no publishing available."

He said, "Well, I can't cut it then."

The publisher of a song owns the copyright, so there was no way I was going to let someone else have the publishing.

After that, I thought I had better do something different. I drove up to Bakersfield and walked into Buck Owens's office. I had met Buck before. I played the song for him and he said, "Oh, man, that's good. Let old Blue Book have the publishing and I'll cut it for you." Buck had formed his own publishing company, Blue Book Music.

I said, "No, sir. There's no publishing available."

"Well, I'm not going to put you in the publishing business."

I got mad and told him, "I'll tell you what, I'll just show it to Ray Charles."

He said, "All right, smart aleck, show it to Ray Charles."

Buck stood in the doorway and watched me walk across the street to a phone booth on the corner. I called Piggy Smith, Keely's brother, because I knew he had every phone number in town. He gave me Ray Charles's office number, and I called it from that phone booth. Mike Akapof answered the phone and said I could have an appointment at 10 the next morning.

Ray Charles's office was in downtown Los Angeles on Washington Street. Mike met me at the door, and when I walked in, I noticed that the walls didn't go all the way to the ceiling. I thought, "What a funny way to build a building."

We had to show the songs on acetate discs in those days. Mike put the needle down on that acetate and played through the first verse. The phone rang; Mike answered it and said, "Yes, sir, I'll do that," and hung up. He turned to me and said, "If you'll give us a one-year exclusive on this song, I'll guarantee you the A-side of a Ray Charles single."

I said, "Put that in writing."

He walked out to the secretary, had her write it up, and brought it back to me. I said, "Okay, we'll do that."

Ray, of course, was sitting on the other side of one of those walls that didn't go all the way to the ceiling. He had heard every word we said, and he had heard that demo on that acetate.

That was in August 1966. In May of 1967 Ray released that song and it went to number one in the R&B charts, although it only went to number five in the pop charts. Then Nancy Sinatra cut it. Lee Hazlewood was recording her, and he was a good friend of ours, so she had a single with it the next year that went into the top 20. The year after that, Dean Martin had a single with it that also went into the top 20. We had three singles, three years in a row.

Glen Campbell cut it on one of his first albums, and then Bobby Goldsboro recorded it. Jimmy was recording Frankie Laine, so he cut it, and years later George Strait released it. In all, it was recorded sixty-three different times.

A couple of years later, Donnie and I wrote some more songs that we thought Ray might like, and when I got to his office, the receptionist remembered me. She said, "Oh, Red, come on in. Mr. Charles will be with you in just a minute." She took me back into the studio, pointed at a chair, and said, "It would be best if you sit there."

I sat down and in a little bit I could hear Ray shuffling down the hall. He was counting his steps, and I could tell that he knew where the step up into the studio was. He walked to the edge of the soundboard, put his hand on it, reached back and got a chair, pulled it under him, and said, "Now, what have you got, Red?"

I played him a couple of songs and he said, "Well, they're good. But they're not quite what I need. Sure do appreciate you coming by."

I was overwhelmed by the fact that he remembered who I was and that he gave me that time. Several years later he was playing at the Western Place in Dallas. I was in Dallas at the time, so I decided to go see him. His manager, Joe Adams, was up front taking tickets when I walked in and he said, "Does Ray know you're here?"

I told him that he didn't, and he said, "Let's go talk to him."

Joe had somebody else take over what he was doing and we went around back to this big GMC motorhome. We stepped in the door of that motorhome and Joe said, "Ray, you remember Red Steagall?"

Immediately, Ray sang the first line to "Here We Go Again" and laughed. Then he said, "Red, you are a coward, the biggest that I've ever seen."

I asked him, "Why do you think I'm a coward, Ray?"

"Because you never brought me no more hits."

I said, "I never did write one that I thought was good for you."

He got the biggest kick out of that, just slapped his knee. I'll never forget that as long as I live. My heart was pounding out of my chest to know that Ray remembered who I was and that that song had meant that much to him.

When we got Ray to record that song, I was still working for the chemical company because I didn't know very much about the music business. But I was hanging out with Jimmy and Donnie and their friends, and Jimmy was allowing me to go to all his sessions and watch what was happening so I could learn. Then one day Eddie Reeves, a friend I had known in college, called.

Eddie had grown up in Amarillo and had started singing, playing guitar, and writing songs while he was in high school. He had a little band, and they recorded two singles at Norman Petty's studio in Clovis. A couple of years after Eddie got out of college, Norman hired my friend as his New York representative, and about a year later he went to work for United Artists Music in New York. Eddie knew I had gone to California. He called and told me United Artists needed a man in California and wanted to know if I was interested. I was.

There were two parts to my job with United Artists. First, I was a representative of the company, and I would sit in on the dubbing sessions when they were dubbing the soundtracks of United Artists movies. I didn't have any responsibilities; I couldn't say anything, or be critical, but I represented the company. I just sat in a chair and listened. When the movie was finished, I would screen it for recording executives in the hope that they would use the music from the soundtrack to record with their artists. In those days, the movie production company owned all the copyrights, and if they could get the movie scores recorded and released by some well-known artists, it was a good revenue source.

One of the movies that United Artists released during my time with the company was *Live for Life*, and the soundtrack was a marvelous Paul Francis Webster and Francis Lai score. Two other movies with great music during that time were *In the Heat of the Night* and *Midnight Cowboy*.

I learned a lot while I was doing this, but where I really learned about the business was when I officed next door to Burt Lancaster.

My office with United Artists was a little bungalow on the Samuel Goldwyn Studios lot, across from the commissary, and Burt Lancaster was next door to me. He also had a little bungalow, but he had a porch with some rocking chairs. I would see him out there, and he would wave at me through the window. I would go sit in one of his rockers, and he would tell me stories. At 3 in the afternoon, we would go to the commissary and have some vanilla ice cream with maraschino cherries on it. That was our deal.

Occasionally, he would say, "They're shooting a piece of a television show that you might enjoy. Let's go watch it." We would walk around the sound stage and he would tell me exactly what was happening, what each person was doing, and why some of them were just standing around with their hands in their pockets instead of working.

"They're waiting until somebody says, 'Move that shrubbery,'" he told me. "That's the green man. He's responsible for the shrubbery and he's the only one who can touch it." He taught me all kinds of stuff about the movie and television business, just walking around on that sound stage with him, and I did that day after day.

This was back in the day of the big bands, like Hugo Montenegro and Percy Faith and all the others, and I had gotten "Live for Life" cut thirteen times. They were all doing it. One day my boss in New York—not Eddie, but someone else—called me and said, "I need a single on 'Live for Life.'"

I told him, "I've gotten it cut thirteen times and you're going to make a lot of money out of it. I can't beat them about the head and shoulders and have them release it as a single."

He asked, "Do you know Jimmy Bowen?"

I said that I did, and then he asked me if I knew Jerry Fuller, Dick Glasser, and Lee Hazlewood, all of whom were top record producers in Hollywood at the time. I told him that I did.

"You tell those boys that your job at United Artists depends on you having a single on 'Live for Life.'"

I held the phone way out at the end of my arm and hollered, "What effing job?!" hung it up, and walked away.

I wasn't just cocky, I was belligerent and bulletproof. People were cutting songs for me, and I wasn't going to let somebody run over me like that. Besides, I had just gotten my first check for "Here We Go Again," $19,000, and I thought I was wealthy.

I went straight to Jimmy Bowen's office and told him that I had just quit my job at United Artists. He said, "Good, you just picked up another one. Let's start our own publishing company."

Jimmy was so powerful. He was responsible for the vast majority of the hit records at that time, I mean big hits. I moved into his office space, and I signed a bunch of writers and pitched a lot of songs, got a lot of records cut.

Jimmy owned Amos Records, Amos Productions, and Amos Publications. I ran the publishing company, and we had several writers, two of whom were Kim Carnes and her husband Dave Ellison. Kim Carnes had a big record called "Betty Davis Eyes" that Jimmy produced and was on our label, and Jimmy was still producing Dean Martin, Frank Sinatra, Keely Smith, Buddy Greco, and lots of other acts.

We also represented a writer named Baker Knight who had written quite a few things for Dean Martin. He was a very successful writer, and I pitched a lot of his songs to acts that were more pop oriented. His best-known compositions were "Lonesome Town," "The Wonder of You," and "Don't the Girls All Get Prettier at Closing Time." His songs have been recorded by Ricky Nelson, Paul McCartney, Dean Martin, The Champs, Elvis Presley, Frank Sinatra, Perry Como, Mickey Gilley, Sammy Davis Jr., and Jerry Lee Lewis.

One afternoon, Donnie Lanier, Jimmy, and I were sitting in Jimmy's office, listening to songs for Dean. We would sometimes go through 500 to 600 songs to find ten to show to Dean.

We were listening to songs and drinking a good, white French wine that we ordered by the case. Jimmy's secretary, Bonnie Williams, came in and said, "My son and some more of those kids have left the New Christy Minstrels and they want to record on their own. Would you listen to them?"

Jimmy asked, "Red, do you want to listen to them?"

"Sure," I said.

He told Bonnie, "We'll listen to them sometime."

She said, "Well, they're out in my office right now."

Bonnie brought them in, and it was Kenny Rogers, Thelma Lou Camacho, Mike Settle, and Terry Williams, who was Bonnie's son. They started singing and blew Jimmy away. He called Mike Post, a friend who was also a record producer, and he listened to them. Mike signed them immediately. Jimmy had just gotten a song from Mickey Newbury called "Just Dropped in (To See What Condition My Condition Was In"). Mike Post cut that song with them and that was their first single. They became known as the First Edition, and later Kenny Rogers and the First Edition.

Thelma left the group before too long, and Mary Turner, who wound up marrying Roger Miller, joined it. Mike Settle then left the group, and Kin Vasey took his place. They had lots of hits.

My best friends at that time were Mac Davis and Glen Campbell. We used to play a golf tournament called the Music Man Tournament down in Palm Springs. For several years, we rented a suite that had four sleeping rooms and a sitting area to which all the rooms opened. One evening we were headed to eat supper, and as we started toward the door, I saw Campbell still sitting at the table. I said, "Glen, aren't you going to supper with us?"

He looked up and said, "Red, I can't. If I go out to a restaurant, I can't eat a bite."

That was the first time we realized what a superstar he was.

Before that, I guess I knew things were really happening for him, because we used him on every session that Jimmy did, three times a day, five days a week. He was a guitar-playing fool. He called me one day and asked, "What are you doing this week?"

I said, "Nothing."

He said, "Well, I just got hired to play the Ban-Dar Club in Ventura with Johnny and Jonie Mosby. I need to go up there every night and then be back in time for my early morning sessions. Would you mind driving me up there?"

I told him I would be glad to do it. One evening, we were driving along and "Gentle on My Mind" came on the radio. I said, "Campbell, how does it feel to have a hit record?"

He said, "I don't know if it's a hit or not, but it's got my price up to $300 a night."

About a month later, he was pulling in $30,000 a night plus a percentage of the gate.

Then Glen's career just mushroomed. Jimmy had a company membership at Lakeside Golf Club in Toluca Lake. It was founded by Randolph Scott, Bing Crosby, Bob Hope, and Gene Autry, and their names were on the logo of the club. Glen became such a superstar overnight that they changed the logo so they could add his name.

I played golf at Lakeside with Glen Campbell, Jimmy Bowen, and Mac Davis. We would go there for lunch and then play golf in the afternoon, and because of that I got to know Gene Autry, Pat Buttram, Roy Rogers, and lots of others. Gene lived down the street from the club and I saw him almost every time we were out there for lunch.

Several times I was at the Golden Boot Award, which honors actors, actresses, and crew members who made significant contributions to Westerns in television and film, and I spent a little time with Gene and Roy there. In later years, I was asked to emcee that award show, which was quite a feather in my cap.

We had a lot of good times, a lot of interesting times growing up in the industry, but I didn't think I was in an industry. We would all go to Nancy Sinatra's house and go swimming in the afternoons. She would have a big bunch of hors d'oeuvres delivered. We had great times doing things like that, and they were just my friends. I didn't think about them as superstars until they couldn't do the things we did before.

We played six-man football in Jimmy's backyard. He had a big backyard on Toluca Boulevard where he lived in Toluca Lake, and we all loved football.

Some of the executives down on Hollywood Boulevard, and big stars, actors, singers, and musicians, would put their teams together and come challenge the boys from Texas. We met some of the most wonderful people playing six-man football. I was not very effective as a one-armed football player, but I was part of the team.

There were two neighboring backyards along Jimmy's fence. One of them belonged to Lee Hazlewood, and one belonged to Andy Griffith. They were our referees. I just loved Andy Griffith. I thought he was the funniest guy I ever knew.

One time, Jimmy and I walked over to talk to Lee, and Jimmy said, "Lee, I need to record Nancy Sinatra. If I do, Keely will kill me, and I'm afraid Frank will kill me if I don't." Then he asked, "Would you produce her?"

Lee said, "Sure."

Lee called back the next day and said, "I have the song, everything." That night, he had written "These Boots Are Made for Walkin.'" Nancy recorded it and it reached number one in both the United States Billboard Hot 100 and in the UK Singles Chart.

I had a lot of experiences like that. I think back on them now, and they were monumental. At the time, they were just commonplace because that was my world. I didn't know to be anxious or intimidated, because those were my buddies. We played golf together.

Jimmy is one of the greatest psychologists I've ever known. He bought a Winnebago motorhome, and when some guys would come down from New York to try and make a deal with him, he would say, "Well, let's drive over to the other side of town and talk about it."

He had a driver named Bud who, as it turned out, was a good cook. We would get fifty miles up the coast highway, and Bud would stop and cook some steaks in a park. We would all eat, and by then, Jimmy would have the deal done. He made lots of deals in that Winnebago. He's a genius at putting things on his own turf.

Tex Williams, who was an old-time Western swing musician—he did "Smoke! Smoke! Smoke!" back in the '40s—had a place over in Santa Clarita Canyon, and Steve Stone, who was a songwriter and record producer, had a place right across the hill from me. I lived in Lost Canyon, in the Sand Canyon area, in Santa Clarita. Steve would ride his horse to my house, and we would ride through the Disney ranch to Tex's house.

Tex had a hitching post along the creek at the back of his house, and we would tie our horses there, go sit on his back porch, have a drink, and listen to him tell stories. When it got dark, we would ride back to the house. We did that dozens of times.

Monte Hale was an old-time Western film star and a musician, and he was a good friend. He held court at the Sportsman's Lodge every single day for lunch. He would have a whole bunch of pocketknives—those little cheap pocketknives that he had made—and he would give them away to all the kids that came by. We would sit there and listen to his stories about the movie business.

Ernest Borgnine was a real close friend, and I just loved Ernie to death. Harry Carey Jr., a great, great actor, was a good friend. I was very close to Ben Johnson, and Wilford Brimley was like my brother, as was Richard Farnsworth. But they're all gone. Where they lived in my world is a real empty place now, because they were grand gentlemen. They were good friends and great actors, and we all looked through the same window.

One of my closest friends was Mac Davis. Mac loved to ride horses. After I moved out into Lost Canyon, we could ride our horses just about anywhere we wanted to. Mac would come out and if I didn't have anything for him to ride, we would rent him one from a riding stable that was close by.

When I lived in Sepulveda, Mac was at my house nearly every weekend. One time, he was out there, and I was working on some mulberry trees with a chainsaw. They hung out over the swimming pool in the backyard, and they were nasty; they would fill the pool with leaves. He didn't want to get close to that chainsaw, that wasn't his deal, so he was sitting in the living room. I finished most of my tree trimming and he comes out with his guitar, sits down on the edge of the pool with his feet in the water, looks up at me, and says, "I just finished one that I think you'll like." He sang "In the Ghetto."

Mac had been working for Metric Music, writing and pitching songs to other artists. Nancy Sinatra formed Frank & Nancy Music, and Billy Strange was running the company. They offered Mac a deal that he couldn't turn down, so he signed with them. Then Billy Strange was hired to do the next Elvis Presley film. Mac had three songs, "In the Ghetto," "Don't Cry Daddy," and "Memories," and Presley cut all three of them. All of a sudden, Mac was the hottest songwriter in Hollywood.

Mac's office was right above mine at 9000 Sunset Boulevard, and we had lunch together every day. One day, we were standing on the sidewalk, waiting for the traffic to clear so we could cross the street and get a hamburger, and this big limousine with blacked out windows rammed up to the curb in front of us.

The door of the limousine opened and this voice said, "Mac Davis, you're the best damn songwriter in America." The door slammed shut and away they went.

I was standing a little over to the side, but the door opened right in front of Mac. After the limousine pulled away, he asked, "Was that him?"

I said, "That was him. That was Elvis."

That was the first time I had been near Elvis since I was on that show with him in Amarillo while I was in college. He and Mac ended up becoming good friends.

Mac was an amazing human being. I'll be forever indebted to him for all the things he taught me and the way he enhanced my life.

Another thing that made a big difference in my life, although I didn't realize it at the time, was meeting Bob Kingsley when I first got to Hollywood. Bob rose to national prominence in 1974 when he became the producer of the nationally syndicated "American Country Countdown," a weekly internationally syndicated radio program that counted down the top 40 country songs of the previous week. We all gathered at Martoni's, a restaurant and club that Frank Sinatra had built for a couple of his friends from Sicily, Mario and Tony, and it had incredible Italian food. We spent lots of evenings there.

One day, Bob said to me, "I joined this group that I think you'd enjoy. It's called the Academy of Country and Western Music. We have a meeting tonight and I want you go with me."

I went to the meeting with him, and there was Gene Autry and Roy Rogers, and over on the other side of the room was Eddie Dean and Jimmy Wakely, both of whom were actors and singers in some of the old Western movies, and there were a whole lot more. I jumped right in the middle of that, and once a month, I would be at that meeting with those guys.

From the very beginning, I became friends with nearly all of them. We would go over to Jimmy Wakely's house, sit on the floor, and pass a guitar around. Everybody would show what they had been writing. This is called a guitar pull. The "pull" part comes from the assumption that there was only one guitar among the group, so one may have to "pull" it away from another in order to get a turn.

Joining the Academy changed my life, broadened my horizons, and gave me contacts in areas that I would never have been able to get into otherwise. It was very educational, it was exciting, and it made me want to do a better job. It gave me ideas about what kinds of things to write, not trying to be competitive but trying to be as good as that person over there who was getting all his songs cut.

What is it about his songs that mine don't have? It helped me to criticize and evaluate my writings.

Later, I was incredibly fortunate to be the chairman of the Board of Directors for that institution, and then we changed the name to the Academy of Country Music in order to compete better with the Country Music Association in Nashville.

Bob Kingsley also liked to ride. He had a horse at Griffith Park on the Burbank side of the river. I would go out there and rent a horse from the stables. We would ride across that river and up into those hills as often as we could, get out of that mess below.

That's when I got to know Richard Farnsworth, Wilford Brimley, and Ben Johnson. Ben was one of the dearest friends I'll ever have, and a man who influenced me an awfully lot.

Besides being an actor, Ben was a former world champion team roper, and he started having benefit team ropings to raise money for cystic fibrosis. All those cowboy actors loved to rope, and we raised millions of dollars for children with cystic fibrosis.

The first time I ever saw Ethan Wayne, John Wayne's youngest son, he roped with me at one of our ropings. On the first run he made, he caught two heels. He was so tickled I thought he was going to die; that was the greatest thing that ever happened to him. I see him occasionally, and we still laugh about that. It was something special to us because we were part of the cowboy life, and here Ethan's father was John Wayne, the iconic cowboy actor.

The only time I ever met John Wayne, I really didn't meet him, but I had a friend who was producing the spoken-word album *America, How I Love Her* that the actor recorded. My friend had a little studio on Hollywood Boulevard, upstairs, above a store. He came by my office one day, and told me, "I'm about to finish that album with John Wayne. He'll be in the studio in about an hour if you'd like to come see him."

I was scared to death. I sat across the table from him and watched them do *America, Why I Love Her*, and I never spoke to him. I was in awe, and I was afraid that I would offend him with anything that I said.

Rex Allen was a dear friend. Rex told me lots of stories about how he got started and how life was for him, and later, we did a lot of shows together, rodeos and fairs and things like that. I just thought the world of him.

The actor Robert Fuller (we called him Bob) is as close a friend as I'll ever have. Bob had a good friend, Carl Mills, who had a hunting preserve southwest of Bakersfield. Bob and I, Glen Campbell, Dave Burgess, and Bob Kingsley would go up there on the weekends just to get out of Hollywood and hunt some birds. Dave had some good Brittany dogs, and I loved to hunt over those dogs.

One weekend, Jerry Fuller went with us. Jerry was originally from White Settlement, Texas, but he had moved to California and became a very good and important record producer, singer, and songwriter. The first night we were there, we got into the whiskey pretty good, and Bob Fuller said, "Jerry, I'll bet we're kin since we've got the same last name."

Jerry looked over at him: "I don't know, I'm from Texas."

Bob said, "Well, I'm from Florida, but I had some people that moved to Texas one time."

Jerry asked, "Does Clarence ring any bells?"

"No."

"How about Claude?" Jerry asked.

Bob shook his head no.

"Jeremy?"

Again, Bob said no, and they went on all night long, drinking whiskey and still coming up with names that didn't fit. About sunup, Bob Fuller looked at Jerry Fuller and said, "Jerry, we can't be kin."

Jerry said, "The hell we can't, we have the same last name."

Bob said, "Yeah, I know, but I just remembered, when I got to Hollywood, I changed my name to Fuller."

They had spent all night long trying to figure out how they were related. I have told that story lots of times.

There were a whole bunch of those kinds of folks. I was peddling songs and getting them cut, and I knew nearly everybody in town. Hanging out with them didn't seem that big of a deal. It was just a good time, and I took it all in stride.

CHAPTER 6

BUILDING A CAREER

While I was working with Jimmy Bowen, my job was to look for songs and songwriters, and I had a pretty good stable of them. But I also started going to Nashville and pitching some of my own songs to Nashville recording artists like Del Reeves. I had two number one records with Del, one called "A Dozen Pairs of Boots" and another called "Walk All Over Georgia." I had a song cut by Brook Benton that got into the top 10 in the pop charts, and I wrote a couple of songs with O. C. Smith that paid a lot of bills in those days.

I was getting a lot of my songs cut, and then one day Jimmy asked me, "What do you want to do? Do you want to be a publisher?"

I told him, "Jimmy, I've always dreamed of being a country singer."

He said, "Well, get you a record deal."

Every producer in town knew me because I was pitching songs all the time, so I started making some calls. Jimmy swears he didn't have anything to do with it, but the next day I had three offers, one from Ken Nelson at Capitol Records, one from Joe Allison at Dot, and one from Joe Johnson at 4 Star Records. I went back to Jimmy, looking for advice, and told him I didn't know what to do.

He asked, "Which one do you like the best?" I told him it was Joe Allison. He said, "Joe just got that job with Dot, go with him."

I called Ken Nelson at Capitol Records and told him I was going with Joe. He said, "Red, Joe is going to do you a real good job and then one day he'll disappear and be gone for a while, and he'll lose his job. And in all probability, whoever's going to run that label is going to let you go because you were Joe's guy. When that happens"—he said "when," not "if"—"come back over here and I'll sign you to Capitol."

The first record I did on Dot was "I'm Going Home to Birmingham with an Alabama Woman on My Mind," that Donnie Lanier and I had written. Joe Allison produced it and it was climbing the charts. When it got to about number 30, Joe disappeared and lost his job at Dot. They hired Jim Foglesong to come to Nashville from New York to replace him.

I knew Jim because when I was working with Jimmy Bowen, he had been pitching me songs to show to Dean Martin and Frank Sinatra. Jimmy had been letting Donnie and me do most of the initial casting for Dean and Frank. When he got to Nashville, Jim called me in and said, "Red, I know you as a publisher and I think that's what you are at heart. I've got to trim this roster and I'm going to have to let you go."

I said, "My gosh, Jim, 'Going Home to Birmingham' is climbing the charts."

He said, "Yeah, but I don't think it's sustainable. And I don't think you have what it takes to go forward with it."

So, he let me go. I was devastated, but I got back to Hollywood and walked into Ken Nelson's office.

"It happened, didn't it?" he said.

"Yes, sir."

He handed me a contract. "Take this contract to your lawyer and have him look it over."

I said, "I don't need a lawyer, show me where to sign."

I signed a three-year deal with Capitol and started recording. In the beginning, Ken assigned a couple of first-time producers to me that didn't know a whole lot about the business, and we weren't getting much done. He was trying to indoctrinate them as well as get me started. But one day he called and said, "Joe Allison showed up in Nashville and I put him in charge of the Nashville office. Why don't you record with him again?" Boy, I was thrilled to death.

In 1969, I had written a song called "Beer Drinking Music" that Ray Sanders had recorded and took to number one. Now it was 1972, and Joe said, "Why don't we cut 'Beer Drinking Music' again? It's been long enough." We did, and we got a top 40 record with it.

Then we did "Party Dolls and Wine," and it went into the top 10, and we did "Somewhere My Love" in a Western swing style. Instead of 3/4 time it was 4/4 time, and, boy, you can dance to it. And it was a top 10 record. We did a whole album of those old pop tunes, did them Western swing style, and that may be my favorite album. We had lots of fiddles and guitars in it.

In 1971, "Party Dolls and Wine" was climbing the charts, and I was invited to be on the Grand Ole Opry. Charlie Walker introduced me. I was playing an Ovation fiberglass guitar. It had a spruce top on it, but the body was fiberglass. Just as I got to the microphone, the pin came out of the guitar strap, the strap came off my shoulder and the guitar hit the floor. However, because of that fiberglass, it bounced back up into my arms. I caught it and started playing. Everyone in the audience thought it was part of my act.

That was a long way from Sanford, Texas, and that Arvin radio sitting on top of our Servel refrigerator, plugged into the only electrical outlet in the house. There were many Saturday nights that I sat in that dark kitchen in a cane-bottom chair listening to Charlie Walker on the Grand Ole Opry, dreaming of being on that stage.

I never thought too much about trying to be a member of the Opry. In those days, if you were a member, you had to appear on stage in a certain number of Saturday night performances, and I couldn't afford to do that. I was on the road all the time, and Saturday nights were my only paydays. We didn't work during the week unless it was a special event like a fair opening or a multiple-day rodeo. The rest of the time, it was on the weekends.

Fifty-one years later, I got to play the Opry again. In 2022, my friend Larry Gatlin invited me to be on the Opry as part of a show he was hosting. He wanted me to do "Here We Go Again" and "Lone Star Beer and Bob Wills Music," and he wanted me to do a poem. There had never been a poem done on the stage of the Grand Ole Opry. I did "Born to This Land" and got a standing ovation, the only standing ovation of the evening. My wife Gail was there with me, sitting at the back of the stage, and I don't think either one of us realized how exciting it was until it was all over.

Another of the great moments in my life as a songwriter was when I got to stand by Walter Brennan and direct him when to come in with the music for a song that I had written. Walter Brennan was one of my all-time heroes, and Snuff

Coleman County Cowboys. Front row (L–R): Danny Steagall, the late Rick Solomon, Larry Reed, Don Miller, unidentified officer. Back row (L–R): Unidentified officer, me, the late James Wood, Junior Pruneda, the late Danny McGonagill, and two unidentified officers, circa 1970s.

L–R: The late Mark Abbott, Steve Solomon, Danny Steagall, Lynn Massey, me, Jim Pack, and Buck Reams on stage at Billy Bob's Texas.

Garrett, who produced Walter's albums, had asked me to write a song for an album Walter was doing. I wrote "Rocking Chair Trucker," and Snuff loved it. Then, when I got to direct Walter as he was recording it, it just meant the world to me. That's the only time I was ever around Walter, but I've never forgotten it.

When I first started touring, I put together a band I called the Coleman County Cowboys. I had my brother Danny playing rhythm guitar, Danny McGonagill on drums, James Wood on the steel guitar, Randy "Snuffy" Elmore playing fiddle, and Derald Hicks on bass guitar. They were all very good musicians. Our driver was a friend from Tennessee named Don Miller.

In the early days, we didn't have a bus. I bought a Dodge van and a little 5-foot by 7-foot trailer that we used for about a year, driving all over the country, doing concerts and promoting my records. Then, we were getting enough dates that I thought we could justify a little bus, so I bought a GMC motorhome that we used to pull the trailer.

In 1975, I bought a 1965 Continental Trailways bus. We had it gutted and totally rebuilt the interior with eight bunks, my stateroom in the back, a bathroom, and a salon up front with a couch and a couple of chairs. That old bus wasn't a very good one, but it got us around over the country and we drove it until 1983.

In 1983, Gail and I bought a brand-new Silver Eagle bus and Gail designed the interior. It was beautiful. But about that time country music changed, and we started having trouble getting jobs. By 1985, we had sold that bus and quit living in one. But we had some great times. We covered the country from coast to coast and border to border, living in a bus about 250 days a year.

I'm proud to say that in those days I had one of the best Western swing bands ever put together. My brother Danny was still playing rhythm guitar, Tommy Nash played lead guitar, and on fiddles, at different times I had Ricky Solomon, Stevie Solomon, and Snuffy Elmore. Dale Bruce played bass, Lynn Massey was on drums, Larry Reed played sax, and Wayne Glasson was on piano. That band was together for several years, and we played all over the country. Our road manager was Jim Hammon, who was killed in 1991. He was on the airplane with Reba McEntire's band when it crashed.

Later, some of those musicians were switched out. Gary Carpenter played steel guitar off and on for years, and Rich O'Brien, one of the great guitar players of all time, played with me for twenty-five years or more. Rich passed away in 2023. Today, Danny, of course, still plays with me, Kevin Taylor plays drums,

Three of the best musicians I could ever hope to work with and three of the best friends I could ever imagine (L–R): Steve Story, the late Richard E. O'Brien, and my little brother Danny Steagall.

Jimmy Don Pack plays bass, and Steve Story plays fiddle. Most of our dates today are cowboy shows and I usually take four players, Danny, Jason Roberts, Steve Story, and Dale Burson.

In addition to the band, there are two other people in the music business who have made a difference in my life. Donald J. Williams was my manager for a lot of years, and we had some good times together. Ray Bingham of Claremore, Oklahoma, booked nearly all my dates over my entire career. Both of those gentlemen were professionals, but they were also the best friends a man could possibly have.

•

For about three years, I recorded several songs that got lots of airtime and sold lots of records. Then, in 1975, Joe Allison disappeared again.

Once again, I went back to Jimmy Bowen, asking for his advice. He said, "Call Glenn Sutton."

Glenn Sutton was a songwriter and an independent record producer. He was married to Lynn Anderson, and he cut all her hits. I called Glenn and we started looking for songs.

In those days, the Disc Jockey Convention was the biggest thing in country music. Every country music radio station in America would send a representative to Nashville for the convention, and each record label would have a concert so all their artists could present any new songs they were about to release. I came in off the road for the convention, and as soon as it was over, I drove the bus to Glenn's office, parked right out front.

He played me about four songs, and I told him, "Glenn, I don't like any of those."

Irritated, he asked, "Well, what the hell do you want?"

I said, "My audience wants a song they can drink beer and dance to."

He got aggravated then and said, "Well, how about Lone Star beer and Bob Wills music?" just off the top of his head.

We wrote the song "Lone Star Beer and Bob Wills Music" at 4:00 that afternoon, in about ten minutes, and cut it at 6:00.

Sometimes the magic works that way, but for most of them, you really have to work.

In the meantime, since Joe had disappeared again, Ken Nelson had hired Frank Jones to run Capitol in Nashville. Glenn and I cut the *Lone Star Beer and Bob Wills Music* album, and that was the first album I had done that Joe didn't produce. I went in to see Frank at Capitol and he told me, "I'm not going to release that single."

Shocked, I asked, "Why not?"

He said, "Because it's about a two-and-a-half-minute commercial for Lone Star beer and the FCC won't allow it to be played on the radio. I'm not going to put money into the promotion, and then have no one play the record."

I got mad and said, "Then why don't you sell me that master?"

He got up from his desk, walked to the vault, handed me the master, and wrote out a contract and a price. I took that master and walked across the street to Jim Foglesong's office at Dot. He bought the whole album. I walked back across the street and handed a check to Frank Jones.

The song went to number five nationally. The only reason it didn't go to number one is because they wouldn't play it in Indianapolis and they wouldn't play it in San Antonio, where the Lone Star brewery is. When the song came out, Pearl Beer, another beer company headquartered in San Antonio, was buying time on the radio stations. Lone Star and Pearl each ran commercials at different times so they wouldn't compete with each other. When it was Lone Star's turn to buy time on the radio stations, the song had already started downhill.

"Lone Star Beer and Bob Wills Music" was a major turning point for me because Lone Star Beer, the company, got behind us and gave me a pretty good chunk of money to be their spokesman and do their commercials.

Glenn Sutton and I loved trains. We came up with the idea that riding in a train caboose would be inspirational and would be a good place to write songs.

In those days, I thought I was bulletproof. If I wanted to do something, I would just jump right in the middle of it and find people who could help me. The only railroad that I knew anything about was the Rock Island because it had a line that came through Sanford when I was growing up. I called the president of Rock Island Railroad and he took my call.

I explained to him who we were and what we did, and that we wanted to ride a long distance in a caboose to see if it would inspire us to write songs. He said, "We can make that happen. We'll put a caboose on a train in Amarillo, and you can ride from there to Memphis."

Glenn and I flew to Amarillo, boarded the train, and headed for Memphis, Tennessee. There were bunks on both sides of the caboose, and there were also little bay windows that stuck out on both sides so that we could see all the way up the train. There was a restroom, but the toilet was just a pipe with a seat on it. One night, it was snowing and the bathroom door came open. Snow blew up through that pipe and covered both of us in our bunks.

When we went through Holdenville, Oklahoma, the station there had a big sign that read, "Welcome Red and Glenn. Keep Singing," and there were a couple of places where people at the station brought out boxes of sandwiches and soft drinks. We felt like we were real celebrities.

The trip was exciting, but we had one problem; we couldn't stay awake. The rhythm of the car on those rails made us sleepy. We were only able to write one song, "I'm Not Your Kind of Girl." Later, that song would be instrumental in the career of one of the most fantastic entertainers of our time.

CHAPTER 7

SUPPORT

I first met Gail Page in 1961, when my cousin, Terry Gene Coleman, introduced me to her as his girlfriend. Gail and Terry got married in August 1963, but Terry was killed in an automobile accident six weeks later. Gail then moved in with Terry's mother, my aunt, Audra Coleman, in Forestburg, which is where most of my father's side of my family still lived. I was very close to my aunt—that's where I got the idea to name my band the Coleman County Cowboys—and in Gail's living there, she continued to be a big part of my extended family. She also became my best friend.

In the late 1960s, Gail was working for Braniff International Airways and came out to California on several occasions to spend time with me. Donnie Lanier and I had a house in Balboa, and I furnished a bedroom for her. We had lots of good times, and I just assumed that we would get married, although I never talked to her about it. I was as green as a gourd about women, and I guess I was probably afraid she would turn me down. But when I got my first royalty check for "Here We Go Again," I made a nonrefundable earnest payment on a house on Coldwater Canyon. It had an Olympic-sized swimming pool in front and it overlooked the San Fernando Valley. I took Gail out to see it, and she said, "This will make a nice bachelor pad."

That broke my heart. She went back to the Dallas–Fort Worth area, and I decided, "Well, that's that." I met Barbara Lee Stitzel, and we married in 1968. We were like oil and water, but I stayed hooked for nine years, and I gained two sons in the marriage, Carl and Steven. In 1969, Gail married an old childhood chum.

Gail's marriage was not good either, and we always kept in touch. We were still best friends through the two bad marriages.

I had moved to California in 1964, and it was awfully good to me because I realized that a person could be as good as they wanted to be, or as bad as they wanted to be, and nobody cared. I loved the people; I hated the town. I couldn't stand its poverty and filth and squalor. And that's what I saw instead of just concentrating on the real good stuff.

In 1973, when I started having some chart action with my records, I decided the place for me to be was Nashville.

When I first got involved with the Academy of Country and Western Music, one of the people I became friends with was Tex Ritter. Maybe it was because we were both from Texas, but we just kinda bonded. I thought Tex Ritter was one of the grandest gentlemen I had ever met in my life, and I still think that. Tex had moved to Nashville, so I called and told him that I thought it was time I moved there. He said he would help me with a banker and a real estate agent. We found a farm in Wilson County, Tennessee, between Lebanon and Murfreesboro, and Tex introduced me to a banker who loved country singers.

We moved in June 1973. The farm had been neglected for several years, but the boys and I cleaned it up. It was a beautiful place to live. It had originally been deeded to Wesley Hancock in 1787 for his part in the Revolutionary War. Wesley was the son of John Hancock, who, of course, was one of the signers of the Declaration of Independence. I was the first person who wasn't a Hancock to have my name on the deed. But what made it even more attractive was that it was only six miles down the road from the farm that my great-grandparents and great-great-grandparents left in 1870 to come to Texas.

It was a grand old farm. All the buildings were made of lumber that had been cut there on the farm. I even found where the sawmill was; I put in a cross fence and went through about two feet of sawdust digging the postholes. The last Mr. Hancock to be on the farm was commissioner of agriculture under two Tennessee governors. When he built a barn, it was built to last.

I never felt entirely welcome in middle Tennessee. I was a newcomer, and I never completely fit in. I brought my horses from California, and I had several mares that I was breeding. But we had barely moved in when I needed to cut my hay fields. They were primarily fescue grass, and I knew from my agricultural background that you can't feed fescue to pregnant mares after the grass

Our wedding at the home of Edith and Darrell Royal in Austin, Texas, August 2, 1977. (Photo credit Tom Elliott.)

has gone to the boot stage, which is when the seed head is still enclosed or has matured. The mare will abort, or the foal will be born with brain damage.

As soon as I could, I was out in the field, on my tractor, cutting hay. I looked up and saw an old yellow Chevrolet pickup bouncing across the field. It stopped right in front of me. This man got out of the pickup, walked over to my tractor, and asked, "What in the hell are you doing?"

"I'm cutting hay," I told him, which I thought was obvious.

He said, "You can't cut hay, the moon ain't right."

I replied, "To hell with the moon, the fescue's going to boot."

He got back in his truck, drove off, and never spoke to me again. I would see him at the hardware store or the feed store, and he would just stick his nose in the air and walk right on by. I owned that farm for ten years and he never spoke to me again.

I really felt like an outsider after that. I folded my tent on Christmas day 1976, moved to Texas, and as soon as my divorce was final in Tennessee, Gail and I were married. I was single for three days.

Rita Gail Steagall is my life mate, my soulmate, and still my best friend. We got married on August 2, 1977, in the home of University of Texas head coach

Darrell Royal and his wife Edith. I can't imagine one minute of my life without Gail, and I know, without a shadow of a doubt, that I am the most blessed man in the camp.

As time went on, both boys joined us in Texas and graduated from high school here. Unfortunately, we lost Carl, the older one, in 2016 to heart failure. Our younger son, Steven, lives here in Texas and is one of our greatest gifts. He is a very successful draftsman who costs out and designs all kinds of steel buildings. He's very talented; he has his own business, and we're really proud of him. His wife, Deborah, is a great treasure to him and a blessing to us all. They make a wonderful couple and have two sons, Louie and Cody. Louie has a son, Darrin, and that makes great-grandparents out of Gail and me.

Carl came to live with us shortly after my divorce from his mother was final. While he was still in school, he decided he wanted to get a job. I told him about a friend's nephew who was making $700 to $800 a week waiting tables and suggested he might try that. He told me, very emphatically, "I'm not going to wait tables in a restaurant!" Next thing we know, he's working in a little Italian restaurant not far from our house.

After he graduated from high school, he moved to California, went to work in a type of pancake restaurant, and worked his way up to manager. Next, he got a job with another restaurant that was a little larger and had a nicer clientele, and he became manager there. Then he went to work for the Claim Jumper restaurant chain and worked his way up to a manager position there.

Then, a group approached him about building his own restaurant. He tried it, but it failed, and he never fully recovered from that. I think that had a lot to do with his untimely death; he just worried too much about it and put too much pressure on himself.

Son Steven left Texas in the '90s to pursue a career in steel fabrication design. He was very successful there in the San Joaquin Valley where he met and married his true love, Deborah Meza. Their decision to move to Texas in 2023 has been a great blessing to Gail and me. We now have many opportunities to enjoy wonderful family time together.

Gail and I have a very nice little ranch just west of Fort Worth. It's not big enough to make a living on, and it's too big to keep clean, but we love it. It's our paradise.

Our office has been on our ranch since 1980. We have one employee, Debbie Bowman, who has been my right arm for more than forty-seven years. There have been lots of ups and downs and she's been through all of them with us. She is not only an employee, she's a very special dear friend. I joke that I have had two wives for forty-seven years, and I couldn't do without either one of them.

It's not just Gail and Debbie. I know I'm the most blessed boy in the camp because I have the greatest support group that a fellow could possibly have in my siblings. We lost my brother Carroll in 2019. But Carroll Leon Steagall was like Daddy in many ways. He could walk into a plant yard and in a very short period tell you exactly how everything in the plant worked. He knew all kinds of ways to distribute liquids and gases, and he was very, very good at it.

When I first went to Hollywood and was selling industrial chemicals for Van Waters & Rogers, we were building a tank for General Film Labs. They had a big film to process, and they were getting low on ammonium thiosulfate 16 percent. I had ordered it and was sure it had been shipped, so I pulled out the bill of lading and called the number on it. Carroll answered the phone. He was in Cactus, Texas, making the ammonium thiosulfate 16 percent for Kerley Chemical Company. I was selling it in Hollywood and neither one of us knew we had that connection.

Carroll wasn't an engineer. He didn't have a college degree, but Bob Kerley totally depended on him to run those plants and knew that he could do a good job of it. Carroll had one son, Bart, and a daughter, Melissa.

My brother Barry, who is married to Barbara, is next in line. Barry Fain Steagall is a businessman, the best of all of us. He always loved engines, while Carroll and I loved horses. He always played with trucks and tractors, and the first thing he did when he got out of high school was buy an old service station there in Sanford. Barry founded Steagall Oil Company in Chickasha, Oklahoma, where he supplied manufactured oil and lubricants to the oil field and to manufacturers of all kinds. He operated the company for forty-six years, but he recently sold it to a larger company and is now retired.

Barry has five children. His son David is married to Keri Ann and they have two daughters, Grace and Lauren. Son Steve McEuen and his wife Janice have two children, Mikayla and Rocky, who is married to Charles Wren. They have two sons, Holden and Zachary. Zachary is married to Maddie, and they have one daughter, Penelope. Barbara's daughter Becky Lewis and her husband, Malcolm, have four children, Kylie, Adam, Rebecca, and Rachelle.

My little sister is the crown jewel in our world. Sue Anne Williams is the kindest, sweetest human being I've ever known in my life, and not just because she's my sister. It's because that's just the kind of person she is. We all just idolize her. She has a wonderful family, and she was Mother's salvation. If it hadn't been for Sue Anne, Mother might not have lasted very long because us three older boys dealt her a lot of misery, just doing things that boys do. Sue Anne was the steadying influence for us kids.

Sue Anne has four children. Her daughter Kimberlee is married to Scott Linder, and they have two children, Carlie and Jackson. Carlie has a daughter, Georgia. Sue Anne's daughter Dava is married to Orrin Thompson, and their children are Afton, who is married to Garrett Sheil, and Chelsea, who is married to Kody Marx. Afton and Garrett have two daughters, Willow and Zoey. Chelsea and Kody have one daughter, Kora, and a son, Colson. Sue Anne's daughter Kristina Lewis has a daughter, Kaitlin, who is married to Mathieu Cerankowski, and a son, Benton. Sue Anne's son Spencer Williams and wife Ashley have sons Curtis and Austin, and a daughter, Hannah.

Next in line is my brother David Lynn Steagall, and David was the general manager of Steagall Oil Company. He also has that same ability that Daddy had to recognize what makes things work and how to handle problems, and he knows how to handle people. He was a very, very good adjunct and complement to Barry's business, and he's a great cowman and horseman, as well. Today, he ranches in south central Oklahoma.

David and his wife, Nancy, have four sons: Stason, Jay, Shane, and Bobby. Stason has two sons: Heath, whose children are Alex and Scarlett, and the late Scott Steagall. Jay is married to Kim, and they have two children, Brennon and Skyllar. Jay is a member of the Oklahoma State House of Representatives. Shane and his wife, Courtney, have three children, Owen, Allison, and Julian. Shane operates his own chemical business in the Houston area. Bobby is active in the IT business and at this point is single.

Last is little brother Danny Mitchell Steagall. I was 15 when Danny was born, and early on, I recognized that he had a tremendous amount of musical talent. When he was 3, I let him play my mandolin, and before long he was playing "These Shoes Keep Walking Back to You." He's always been very musical. He went to college at West Texas State, stayed a couple of years, and then, much to Mother's dismay, went on the road with me in 1976. To this day, he still is on stage with me when I do a concert. Anytime I need to record something musical, Danny is on board. He was a sales manager for Barry at Steagall Oil Company and today works for the new company as a lubricant engineer.

Danny and his wife, Shelia, have three children, a daughter, Chissica Godfrey, and two sons, Jason Adams and Brian Dahi. Chissica's children are Chelsea Castillo, Chase Ramirez, and Emily Godfrey. Chelsea has a daughter, Camille Castillo. Jason has a son, Justus, and Brian and his wife Courtney have a son, Luke Asher Dahi.

I'm so proud of all my brothers, my sister, and their families. They are my support group, I'm their support group, and we have a wonderful life. They all have great families and we're the most blessed people in the world. Mother has been gone for a while, and we all dearly miss her. But we study the things that she taught us and try to live by them and be the kind of people that she would be proud of. I think she would be proud of us all.

CHAPTER 8

RODEO AND REBA

There are several things that have happened in my life that made it take a different direction, and one of them took place the first week of December in 1974. I decided I wanted to get back in the rodeo business; I wanted to be associated with rodeo people. My friend Ernie Taylor invited me to go with him and Walt Garrison to the National Finals Rodeo, which at that time was in Oklahoma City, and I went.

Ernie had been the world champion calf roper the year before, and Walt was the celebrated running back for the Dallas Cowboys and a spokesman for U.S. Tobacco, which was very involved in professional rodeo. The two of them introduced me to lots of cowboys. The National Finals is a week-long event, and the headquarters hotel that year, where all the cowboys stayed, was the Hilton Northwest. One day, I was walking down the hallway in the hotel and I saw some people in one of the rooms watching an eight-second, black-and-white loop on the television. It was running over and over, playing continuously.

There was a little guy sitting in a chair by the door, and everybody was talking to him, asking him questions. I thought, "Maybe that's somebody I should know."

I walked in, sat down beside him, and started talking to him. His name was Freckles Brown. The tape they were watching was of the night he had ridden Tornado.

Tornado was a bucking bull that belonged to rodeo stock contractor Jim Shoulders and had never been ridden. In 1967, at the National Finals Rodeo, Freckles was 46 years old. He drew Tornado and rode him.

I sat there and watched that tape, and that bull was bucking hard. I got to thinking about that, and as I was flying home to Nashville, I wrote the song "Freckles Brown" on napkins the flight attendant had given me.

The following month, January 1975, I went to the Professional Rodeo Cowboys Association convention at the Brown Palace Hotel in Denver. I wanted to talk to some rodeo committees and see if I could book just one rodeo during the coming year, and then maybe later book some more. But while I was there, I got rodeo announcer Clem McSpadden to listen to my song about Freckles.

Clem was one of the best known and most respected announcers in all of rodeo, and he was general manager of the National Finals Rodeo for eighteen years. I had my guitar with me and played the song for him. Then I asked him if I had all the facts right.

"No, not quite," he said. One of the lines in the song said that Freckles wrapped his rope on dark gray hide because I thought Tornado was a Brahman bull. The film that I watched was in black and white. "He was a red bull," Clem said. "He was a Braford."

Then he said, "I think Jim needs to hear this," and he went to find Jim Shoulders. I played the song for Jim, and he started crying. Then Jim said, "Freck needs to hear this." They found Freckles, brought him back to the room, and I played it for him. He started crying.

Heading to the convention that January, I wanted to book one rodeo. I just wanted to get my feet in the pond. Because of that song, I booked nineteen rodeos. For the next seventeen years, I worked thirty-five to forty rodeos a year. Those cowboys became my family. I love all the people in rodeo. Some of the best friends I've ever had in my life were people who were or are a part of the world of rodeo.

Clem was so impressed with the song that the next year he asked me if I would come to the National Finals in Oklahoma City and sing it every night at the rodeo while sitting on the chute gate.

Each performance, when we started, we had the house totally dark, and it was quiet. You could have heard a pin drop. I mean it was total silence in that entire coliseum. I began the song, and then, under a spotlight, Freckles walked out from the far end of the arena with his leggings on, carrying his bull rope. From the side, we released a bull called Osceola, that belonged to Matt Dryden from Florida, and they had a spotlight on him.

Osceola was absolutely gorgeous, and we worked on him for a while, feeding him cattle cubes out of Freckles's hip pocket. He wasn't mean, but he would go looking for those cubes.

We kept Freckles in a spotlight, and on the other side of the arena, we put Osceola in a spotlight. That way it looked like there was a big, deep canyon between them. If it wasn't for that, Osceola would have been right on top of Freckles, looking for those cubes. He got so mad because he could see Freckles over there and he didn't think he could get to him. He would throw dirt up over his back and shake his head. The crowd went absolutely bananas. We did that routine ten nights in a row, and it's one of the most exciting things I've ever done.

I started working a lot of rodeos then. The pinnacle, of course, was that performance at the National Finals in '76, but in 1977, W. R. Watt Jr. hired me to play the rodeo at the Fort Worth Stock Show.

I grew up in the Texas Panhandle, and although it was a six-hour drive from my home to Fort Worth, the Fort Worth Stock Show was the closest major stock show to us, and we thought it was the greatest show on earth. Mr. Watt was general manager of the stock show, and when he called, I thought I had died and gone to heaven. There would never be anything bigger than that.

But then Mr. Watt hired me again in 1979, and in 1996, he hired me to do the Centennial celebration of the Stock Show, which was a huge production.

Tad Griffith put it all together, and that young man is one of the most talented people I have ever known. I came out dressed as a Confederate soldier back home from the war. I was out in the arena horseback, singing and reciting poetry, and the band was over in the corner.

We had a big herd of Longhorns in the arena, and as I sang the song "Little Joe the Wrangler," Mr. Watt's grandson came riding in dressed as a teenage cowboy during the trail driving days.

Then we had a rustler that we caught and hung. There was a harness on him, and when the horse ran out from under him, he dropped, but there wasn't any way he could get hurt. However, some complaints were made about it, so after the first couple of performances, we quit hanging him.

Then there was a chuckwagon that got loose and went across the arena floor, rolled over, and exploded. The driver jumped off the seat of the wagon right before it rolled over. At the end of the show, they would drag the wagon into the alleyway and put it back together, ready for the next performance. All the pieces were hinged together.

For the finale of the show, we had a big glass mirror ball, like you see in ballrooms, only this one was great big, and it had a ramp that came out of it. A girl riding a horse and carrying the American flag came into the arena and she was covered with flashing lights. After she had circled the arena, she rode up the ramp into the ball, the door closed, and they hoisted her up into the ceiling while I was singing the last song. She stayed up there until the rodeo was over.

We did a lot of other dynamic stuff, too, in that celebration show, but those were the things that people remember. It was absolutely the most wonderful show I've ever been a part of.

I was invited back in 1998 to celebrate the Sesquicentennial of Fort Worth, and I returned in 2002 for the rodeo to recognize 9/11. I rode into that arena lots of times. I'm the only person who ever played the stock show five times.

Growing up in the Texas Panhandle, I always thought that if I ever got to play the dances at the XIT Rodeo in Dalhart, Texas, and the Tri-State Fair in Amarillo, I would be at the top. There wasn't anything bigger than those two. When I got to do both of those, I thought, "Boy, you made it." We also played Cheyenne Frontier Days in Wyoming; the rodeo at Pendleton, Oregon; the stock shows in San Antonio, Texas, and Denver, Colorado; and the Cow Palace in San Francisco, all the big ones.

I played a lot of small rodeos, too. But a lot of them didn't have the money to hire an entertainer, so I came up with a plan. I told them, "If you'll have a dance after the rodeo, we'll play the dance too, for the same price, and the money you take in from the dance will pay for us. Then your rodeo performance won't cost you anything." I did that for years.

Wyoming, Michigan (outside Grand Rapids), was a great rodeo. We played the dance there two different years. I had six-year contracts with the Days of '47 Rodeo at Salt Lake City, and at Colorado Springs, and I played each of those rodeos every other year for six years. I played Sydney, Iowa, and it was six days in a row, and Jim Sutton used me a lot up in South Dakota and Wyoming. We played lots of dances.

And every single rodeo we went to, we knew where the radio station in town was. We would pull our bus up in front of the station and go in and talk to the

World Champion Rodeo Cowboy the late Larry Mahan (left) and me.

Me and the guy who held it all together for the late Charlie Daniels, David Corlew (center) and rodeo hero, the late Larry Mahan (right).

disc jockey. Our bus had our name on it, so it was good publicity for us, and it was good for the disc jockey, for the radio station, and for the rodeo promoter.

One time, I was playing the rodeo at Fort Smith, Arkansas. Billy Minick was the stock contractor, and he put me on a big old yellow horse. The plan was for me to come into the arena and circle it, and when I got close to the bandstand, get off and do "Truck Drivin' Man," because that was my hit at the time.

Well, I loped up to the bandstand, and when the band hit the first note, that old yellow horse just stuck his front end in the ground. I came off, did a perfect somersault and landed on my feet. I reached up, got the microphone, and went to work.

After I finished my performance, one of the rodeo committee men came up to me and said, "You have got to come back to the press room. They're just dying to talk to you." I knew what it was about, and I didn't know what I was going to say. I went back there, and there were people with cameras and notepads everywhere. This lady said, "I've got to know, how long did it take you to make that dismount work?"

I said, "Oh, two or three seconds," turned around, and walked out. That's all I told them. I wasn't about to get caught in that trap.

While the band and I were playing all those rodeos, we had the greatest time. We saw the whole country and played to the greatest people in the world, rodeo fans. Because I was at all those rodeos, lots of the cowboys became my buddies, and I saw them several weeks a year. Some of them even traveled on the bus with us at different times. But probably my real introduction to the world of rodeo came in Denver one year.

I had a room at that old round Holiday Inn, where Interstate 25 and Interstate 70 come together, almost at the end of downtown. The room was full of cowboys after the rodeo performance one night. We were singing and drinking beer, and then I noticed they were splitting my beds down, taking the mattresses off the box springs. I had two beds, and all of a sudden, I had four beds.

Then Goat Mayo got up on a chair and said, "Hey, y'all hang on just a minute. Red paid for this room. Leave him a mattress. Don't make him sleep on box springs." They all spent the night in my room, some on the other mattress and some on the box springs.

That was my first real introduction to rodeo cowboys. In the ensuing years, lots of cowboys stayed in the rooms that the band and I rented. We just loved to have them share rooms with us because a lot of them didn't have a dime. They were our buddies. It was a great time.

In 1977, I released a rodeo album called *For All My Cowboy Friends*. It had mostly rodeo songs on it, and one of the songs was "Freckles Brown." Most of the others were songs I came up with while I was talking to rodeo people.

Me and the late Lane Frost.

I got the idea for "Ballad of Dawson Legate" while listening to Clem McSpadden announce a rodeo. Larry Mahan had gotten bucked off over the front end of a bronc and was stepped on. He was just lying there, and the whole coliseum was silent; everyone knew he was hurt bad. As it turned out, he had broken his wrist and collarbone, and the fall had knocked the wind out of him so he couldn't move for a little bit. That was the premise of my song, "Ballad of Dawson Legate," which I wrote on an airplane the next morning. Larry, of course, recovered, but in the song, Dawson Legate is killed when his bronc falls and rolls over him.

Once, I was working the rodeo at Abilene, Texas, and when it was over, I was out in the parking lot talking to Ernie Taylor. Ernie was leaning against his pickup, about to leave, and I asked him if he was headed home.

He said, "Well, I don't know. I think my wife left me." Then he looked at me and said, "I doubt she left much, a pair of boots maybe, a couple pairs of jeans and a trophy saddle."

I couldn't wait to put that story to music. As soon as he drove off, I wrote "Two Pairs of Levi's and a Pair of Justin Boots" right there in the parking lot.

Another song on the rodeo album was "Bandito Gold," which is about a palomino colt that belonged to the young son of a rancher. When things got tough on the ranch, the father had to sell his son's colt. I got the idea for that one when the boys and I were at Lloyd Brinkman's horse sale in Kerrville, Texas, to play for the party after the sale. My brother Danny and I were standing by the door, watching the sale, when they ran a palomino colt into the ring. Next to us was a man holding the hand of his young son. As that colt stood in the ring, the little boy said to his father, "Daddy, buy me that horse. You had to sell mine."

Danny and I went straight back to the bus, and in a few minutes, we had written "Bandito Gold."

I got another song in much the same way, although this one is not on the rodeo album. I had gone to the San Angelo Roping Fiesta one year, and Tooter Shanklin and I were sitting in the shade underneath the announcer stand eating saltine crackers and summer sausage and drinking Lone Star Beer. Tooter was a rancher and a cow man, and he raised polo horses down at Rock Springs, Texas. I asked him, "Tooter, who did you bet on in the Calcutta?"

"I bought this boy from Monument, New Mexico," he said, "and if he ever gets his mind off of something besides neons and nylons, he's going to be a hell of a roper."

He was talking about Roy Cooper, who, of course, went on to win eight world championships. After Tooter said that, I went straight to my pickup, got my guitar out, and right there in the cab of that pickup wrote my song "Neons and Nylons."

The rodeo cowboys had a dramatic effect on what I did and the kinds of songs I wrote. They were my family, and I wouldn't take anything in the world for the experiences I had with them.

In January 1977, my band and I were at the Professional Rodeo Cowboys Association (PRCA) convention in Denver when Jack Roddy and Dale Smith asked me to ride with them down to Colorado Springs to look at a new location for the PRCA headquarters. Jack and Dale were both on the PRCA board of directors, and they told me the decision had been made to move the association headquarters from Denver to Colorado Springs and to also build a museum, which would become the ProRodeo Hall of Fame and Museum of the American

Cowboy. I started playing dances there at the convention, at my own expense, with all the money going toward building that new museum.

I did that for several years, and I invited other acts to donate their time. I'm not sure how much money we raised, but it evidently meant something to the cowboys. They put me on the advisory board, and my name is on the plaque that's hanging on the wall. It will be there as long as the museum is there, and it's one of the greatest honors of my life.

Also, because of my support all these years and because of that song about Freckles and the album that followed, *For All My Cowboy Friends*, the ProRodeo Hall of Fame, in 2023, selected me as the PRCA Rodeo Legend of the Year.

In 1974, the year I met Freckles at the National Finals Rodeo, I also met someone else there who became a very important part of my life.

At the opening of the rodeo one night, I heard this young girl sing the National Anthem, and I thought she was amazing. Later that evening, after the rodeo performance, I'm walking down the hallway in the Hilton Northwest, carrying my guitar, and this lady comes up and grabs me by the arm. She asks, "Are you going up to the Justin suite?"

Justin Boot Company had a suite every year at the National Finals host hotel, and it became a gathering place for many of the cowboys and cowgirls, especially after the rodeo was over each night. I told the lady that, yes, I was going up to the Justin suite, and she asked, "Can I bring my daughter up there so she can sing with you?"

I was in no position to tell anyone they couldn't come, so I just said, "Sure," and went on up. In a little bit, I was sitting over against the wall, singing cowboy songs, and that lady walked in with this little redheaded, freckle-faced girl hanging on her arm. The lady led the girl across the room and sat her down beside me. The girl started singing with me and it blew me away. I had never heard anybody with that kind of control. Then I realized that was the girl who was singing the National Anthem. Her name was Reba McEntire.

Reba was raised on a ranch in southeastern Oklahoma, and both her father and grandfather were world champion steer ropers. Reba had rodeoed herself, running barrels, but her mother, recognizing her daughter's talent, had encouraged her to sing.

Glenn Sutton and I had written "I'm Not Your Kind of Girl" on our train trip, and I needed somebody to do a demo on it. When I heard Reba, I thought, "Here's an opportunity. I can cut a demo on this girl and have her cut my song." I

Another visit to the beautiful Bell Cross Ranch in Cascade, Montana, with (front, L–R) Gail Steagall, Louise Leathers, Cyndi Brookshire, Mike Rose, and Reba McEntire, and me and Joe Leathers in the back.

L–R: Me and Gail with dear friends Janet and Governor Mike Huckabee at Bell Cross Ranch in Cascade, Montana.

Me with my extra special friend Reba McEntire and her "Sugar Tot" Rex Linn, at Bell Cross Ranch.

found another song in our publishing company that fit, and I had Reba's mother bring her to Nashville. We cut a demo on those two songs.

I started pitching her around town, but in those days, it was difficult to get a girl singer a record deal because girls didn't sell tickets and girls didn't sell records.

One of many headline shows in Las Vegas during the National Finals Rodeo.

Finally, Glenn Keener at Mercury Records said, "Well, I don't like those songs, but I sure like the way that girl sings. Can I sign her?"

I said, "You bet you can sign her."

I had seen plenty of record contracts back when I was working with Jimmy Bowen in Hollywood, so I negotiated that first contract for her, and I stayed with her until that contract was up. Then I hired an attorney to negotiate her next one.

Real early, I used her several times as a supporting act with me and the band, but I never would let her ride the bus. I had nine guys on that bus, and I didn't want it to look bad for her. It just wouldn't have been a good deal. I had her mother bring her everywhere she was booked with me and the band, but there were not a lot of those occasions. There were some pretty good ones, though, and it gave her some visibility, some energy, and some education.

In 1978, U.S. Tobacco hired me as the entertainer at the Copenhagen/Skoal Super Sports Calf Roping in Fort Worth, and I got them to hire Reba as well. Harvey Krantz in Hollywood was a clothing designer that a lot of the music industry stars and celebrities used, and I had just gotten him to make me a new suit. It was denim with maroon insets in the legs and in the coat, and I thought I was pretty flashy. And to top it all off, I wore a maroon shirt that went perfectly with the suit.

Sands Hotel marquee, Las Vegas.

I tucked that shirt inside my white shorts so it wouldn't come out while I was in the arena, but when I stepped off my horse, the zipper on my pants broke and my white shorts were shining. I had no idea that was happening, but when I started singing "My Window Faces the South," people began to laugh. I'm thinking, "What's going on? This is not a funny song."

Reba was not in the spotlight with me at that time, but she walked over to the edge of the light and said just loud enough for me to hear, "Red, your fly is undone."

I looked down and saw that it was gaping wide open. I looked out at the audience and said, "Well, this side has seen it," and I turned to the other side, "y'all might as well see it too."

Poster from the Fort Worth Stock Show and Rodeo 1980.

I took my coat off, and Reba tied it around my waist with the sleeves. I finished that concert, got back on the horse, and rode out of the arena.

Reba is one of the best friends I'll ever have in my life, and I dearly love her. We spend quite a bit of time together, considering where she is and who she is today. She is a wonderful human being and one of the greatest acts that ever walked the face of this earth. She's just my little sister.

In 1977, the first year I played the Fort Worth Stock Show Rodeo, Whistle Ryon had made me a saddle with my name on the cantle. Whistle was Windy Ryon's son, and, of course, Windy was the founder of the famous Ryon's Saddle

Shop in the Fort Worth Stockyards. A local veterinarian loaned me a big, beautiful Paint mare to ride in my introduction into the arena, and I had the boys put my new saddle on that mare.

We played all twenty-nine performances of the rodeo. In the matinee performance on the Tuesday before we were to leave on Sunday to go to Germany, my foot got hung in the stirrup as I was getting off. I fell backward and landed on my back. I jumped up, grabbed the microphone from my bus driver, and started singing.

That next week, we were in Germany, performing at US military bases, and our first stop was Ramstein Air Force Base in Rhineland-Palatinate, a state in southwestern Germany. The band and I were on stage, and this young airman leans over the front of the stage and says, "Hey, Red, I was in Fort Worth last Tuesday when you fell off your horse." It's a small world.

We played several different military bases and officers' clubs on that trip, but two years later, in 1979, we went back to Germany as part of a tour that Marlboro put together. It was us, Faron Young, Tommy Overstreet, Charly McClain, the Osborne Brothers, and the Kendalls. We played in all those old, beautiful concert halls, like in Hamburg and Hanover and Nuremberg.

Those old auditoriums were built long before there was any electricity. Everything was built out of wood, and when you're standing up there performing, the music just surrounds you. It doesn't bounce off the walls, it's just a part of what you're doing. The walls weren't absorbing the sound, they were a part of it. It was the most incredible feeling I've ever experienced on stage.

We played some military bases again, but the vast majority of the shows were for the German people, and they loved us. They were proud of us for being there.

CHAPTER 9

REINVENTING RED

In 1985, country music changed. That was the year sad songs and waltzes quit selling. I still had a good band, and I had a brand-new bus, but I had no place to go. It was like being all dressed up with no place to dance.

One night, I was down in the dumps and went to my office, which is at the entrance to our ranch. I set a record player on the floor and took out all the records that had songs I had written and that had been recorded by other people, singers like Glen Campbell, Dean Martin, Frankie Lane, Bobby Goldsboro, and a lot more, and I sat there all night long and played them.

I realized that I had contributed a goodly amount to the music of America in my lifetime. But I asked myself, "How do you measure success? Do you measure it in the amount of money you've made? Do you measure it by how big the crowds are that you draw, by how many songs you've written that have contributed to America's music? What is success? What's it made of?"

I said to myself, "You're successful. Now what are you going to do? The market that you've known all these years is no longer there. It's a completely different audience, and they're not going to stay tuned in to what you do."

It just so happened that the day before, I had read in *Frontier Times* magazine about a cowboy poetry gathering in Elko, Nevada. My brother Danny was living on my place in a mobile home, so I went down to his house the next morning and asked him, "Do you want to go to Elko, Nevada?"

He said, "Sure, we're not doing anything."

In the beginning, it was called the Elko Cowboy Poetry Gathering, and that first year it featured forty poets and an audience of fewer than 1,000. It was started primarily by Hal Cannon, who is a songwriter, musician, and folklorist, and Waddie Mitchell, a Nevada buckaroo who's one of the best known of all the cowboy poets. It began in 1985 as a place where Western ranchers and cowboys could gather to share poems about their lives working cattle. Today, it's called the National Cowboy Poetry Gathering, and it has grown into a national and international weeklong festival of cowboy poetry, music, and art with its roots in and its focus on the tradition of the cowboy in the West.

Danny and I flew to Salt Lake City, got us a car, and drove to Elko. I'll never forget the first time I walked into the auditorium and this guy was on stage, almost crying. He said, "I thought I was the only person in the world who did this."

The more I talked to those who were there, the more I realized that most of the people who were writing cowboy poetry at that time were putting what they had written in a shoebox on the top shelf of the closet so their grandkids would find it after they were gone. The thought was that writing poetry wasn't the manly thing to do. We went to a couple more of the sessions and listened to different ones recite their poetry, and I thought, "This is where I belong."

I had never allowed myself to write poetry because it took away from my creative juices to write the songs that I was making a living on. But after our trip to Elko, I started writing poetry. For five years, I didn't write any songs; all I wrote was poetry. I sat at my desk and wrote three or four poems a day. They would just pour out of me. It was as if they had been lodged in the back of my mind all those years and were searching for a time to get out. I gave them the time, and I'm proud of the poems I wrote during that period.

There's a story behind the first poem I wrote. Don Malone is a lawyer in Vernon, Texas, and he and I have been friends for years. He grew up on the Waggoner Ranch, which is one of the largest ranches in the country, with approximately 500,000 acres all within one fence. In other words, there is no other property inside the ranch's boundary.

Don had permission to take some of his friends hunting on the ranch, and he invited me and some others. We stayed at what was called the Cedar Top

L–R: Don Malone, Boots O'Neal, me, and Wes O'Neal at the Red River Valley Museum, Vernon, Texas.

Camp, where E. Paul Waggoner had built a big stone hunting lodge. There was a fireplace at both ends, some bedrooms, and a screened-in porch on the south side.

Our hunting trip took place between Christmas and New Year's, and we hunted geese, quail, and feral hogs; had a lot of fun. On Saturday night, the

Waggoner Ranch wagon boss, Jimmy Patterson, and several of the other cowboys came out to partake of our whiskey and food and to play penny-ante poker.

Later in the evening, I was sitting at the poker table, listening to the cowboys talk about working for Waggoner Ranch and about the Waggoner brand, and I realized how loyal they were. When I was young, I was always taught that you give your all to the man who hired you. If a man signs your paycheck, you ride for him and you protect his property, just like it was your own.

Then, Jimmy said, "You know, boys, those are our cattle out there. Yes, the family gets the money, but we're the ones who doctor them, calve them out, brand them, and take care of them. Those are our cattle."

I thought, "What a great way to express their dedication to the man who is signing their paycheck."

Over by the fireplace, sitting in a cane-bottom chair, was a man who had lived at that camp, all by himself, for forty-one years. Paul Whitley couldn't hear it thunder, but he was watching our faces and every time we laughed, he laughed. I thought to myself, "If anybody ever rode for the brand, Paul Whitley rode for the brand."

I got up from that poker table and went outside on that cold December night, leaned against the rail at the edge of the yard, and wrote the poem "Ride for the Brand" in honor of Paul Whitley.

Ride for the Brand

His skin looked like leather,
He walked with a limp
And talked with a slow Texas drawl.
His knuckles were knotted,
His left thumb was gone.
Said a stud bit it off late last fall.

We knew he was lyin',
We watched him dally it up.
But it ain't healthy to call him a liar.
It was Saturday night
Before the wagon went out,
And he was settin' this new kid on fire.

Now, we've all heard his stories
'Bout places he's been,
We all think that Jake's pretty strange.
He looked over at me,
Said, "I'm schoolin' this boy
'Bout the unwritten laws of the range."

The kid was enthralled,
Kinda like in a trance.
Jake sensed that he had a good grip.
He straightened up, hitched his pants,
Took a drink of cold beer,
Turned around with his hand on his hip.

He said, "Son, a man's brand
Is his own special mark
That says 'this is mine, leave it alone.'
You hire out to a man,
Ride for his brand
And protect it like it was your own."

He said, "Mr. Waggoner
Come out here in 1903.
This country was sagebrush, mesquite trees and sand.
He carved him this ranch
Outa blood, sweat and guts,
So be proud that you ride for his brand.

"If you hire out to string bob wire,
Then build him a fence—
Don't matter if it's four or five strand.
Remember, it was you
Who asked for the job,
So don't bitch when you ride for this brand.

"Mr. Waggoner don't
Hold with complainers.
He'll fire one before he can quit.
So if you don't like our outfit,
Then head down the trail,
Find a hoss that your saddle will fit.

"But if you get up early
And catch your own bronc,
Show the boss that you're makin' a hand,
Mr. Waggoner'll be there
To cover your bets
As long as you ride for his brand."

He said, "The winter I spent
At the Sixes,
We had a man at the old Taylor place.
He rode up on some hiders
A skinnin' a cow,
And squared off at them scamps face to face.

"Now he coulda rode off,
Never looked back,
But he just wasn't that kind of man.
We found him in Ash Creek
Shot all to hell.
Nocona Joe died for the brand."

We know the old man
Tells a windy or two,
Like the one about losing his thumb.
And Nocona was killed
In a bar in Fort Worth
By the demons in a bottle of rum.

Bigger than life and special friend, the late Toby Keith (left), with me and one of my best friends (as well as my attorney) Don Ross Malone (right).

Famous cowboy artist, the late Tom Ryan (right), and me at the 06 Wagon in Alpine, Texas.

But I got to thinkin'
'Bout what he had said,
And the more of it I understand,
The more I believe
We'd be all better off
If more people would ride for the brand.

After I recorded the poem, I went back to the ranch and Don Malone and I got Paul in Don's suburban, helped him put in his hearing aids, and played that poem on the CD player. When it was over, Don said, "Paul, what do you think?"

Paul said, "Well, Don, I think Red's pretty windy."

I took that as a compliment.

A couple of months after I wrote the poem, I went to Alpine to the Texas Cowboy Poetry Gathering and I recited "Ride for the Brand" on stage. It was so popular, the next year they used it in their yearbook, which was called "The Brand."

It's kind of a long story, but that poem was instrumental in changing the way I write.

In 1979, I played the rodeo at Filer, Idaho. Sunbeam Clipper Company had a booth in the trade show, and one of the men who was working the booth came out to the bus with a cassette tape in his hand. He said, "A guy gave me this tape and wanted me to give it to you."

I put it in my tape player, and I was overwhelmed with the way this person used the English language and presented a story that you could visually see as you listened to the poem.

There was a phone number on the tape, so when I got home, I called it because I wanted to meet the guy who wrote that way and used the language in the way he used it. He answered the phone and I asked, "Is this Baxter Black?" He said it was and I said, "Baxter, I really like the way you use the language."

He asked, "How do you know about that?"

I told him, "This guy with the Sunbeam Clipper Company gave me a tape that you said to give to me."

"No, I told him to give it to Lynn Anderson. He said that he knew her."

I said, "Well, he probably couldn't find Lynn, so he gave it to me. I'm glad he did because it exposed me to something I wouldn't have heard otherwise.

You don't know me from Adam, but I'd like to spend a little time with you."

He said, "I know who you are."

I went on, "Well, I'm building a new office building on my ranch, and it will be ready in February of next year, 1980. I'd like for you to come out and join us for the opening."

He said, "Oh, I couldn't do that, I've got too much to do. I just wouldn't be able to get away from here."

I could tell that he wanted to come, but he knew he couldn't afford it and didn't want to admit that to me. I told him, "I'll tell you what I'll do. I'll buy you a plane ticket and provide you with a place to sleep, and I'll take the cost of all that out of your first royalty check."

"I'll be there," he said.

The following February, I picked Baxter up at the airport and we immediately became fast friends. He spent about a week with us. I had just finished reading a book of poetry by a fellow named Carlos Ashley, and I loved the way Carlos wrote. The book is called *That Spotted Sow and Other Texas Hill Country Ballads*. I had a screened-in front porch, and Baxter and I sat out there on that porch. I would read a poem out of Carlos's book, hand Baxter the book, and he would read one back to me.

We went through the whole book, and we were both enamored with the way Carlos painted pictures with his words.

After I started writing poetry, I got invited to some poetry gatherings, one of which was in Goodwell, Oklahoma. The first poem I recited there was "Ride for the Brand."

When I began writing poetry, I wrote it the same way I wrote my songs, using what is called sympathetic rhymes. I would use words like home and alone, words that kinda sound alike but don't really rhyme. Baxter was there at that poetry gathering, and as soon as I finished that poem, he came to me and explained that you can't use sympathetic rhyme in poetry. It needs to be strict rhyme, where the latter part of the word or phrase sounds identical to that of another.

I'll never forget this. He pointed his finger at me and said, "Wouldn't you like to know that fifty years from now some English teacher used a piece of your work as an example of how and what we wrote in the time we existed? That won't happen unless you have better discipline in your rhymes than you have now."

I went back and rewrote the poem. What Baxter told me that night created a discipline for me that I hadn't had before, and that's been my guideline ever since. I'm proud of the fact that two of my poems, "Memories in

Me and special friend, the late cowboy humorist Baxter Black, holding his young son, Guy, at Westfest, Copper Mountain, Colorado, in the early '90s.

Grandmother's Trunk" and "The Fence That Me and Shorty Built" have been included in McGraw Hill textbooks.

We lost Baxter in 2022, and I was honored to be a part of a memorial service for one of the greatest guys I've ever known and one of the greatest wordsmiths that ever lived. He was a major part of my life for a lot of years.

Carlos Ashley died in 1993, but before he died, he and I became very close friends; he was probably my greatest inspiration as a poet. In 1990, Baxter and I wrote a poem to Carlos, and those of you who are familiar with Carlos's work will recognize that this poem references some of his poems.

From Me and Baxter

The pictures that you painted
Of those Texas post oak hills
Have changed the way we look at life somehow.

Like the day we sat on my front porch,
Marveled at your rhymes,
And read each other "That Old Spotted Sow."

We've had that wondrous bill of fare
In Bob Sears' chili joint,
Seen Aunt Cordie ride the devil 'cross the hill,
Relived childhood moments
In Jim Watkins' barber shop,
And rode with that old freighter Black Snake Bill.

We've hunted coon and possum
With Edgar Martin's hounds.
We've laid beside the embers with Old Blue
And stood along the rail
While they pounded down the stretch,
As Bonnie beat 'em all in twenty-two.

Friend, you're our inspiration.
You're a sort of guiding light.
You take the time to make the flowers grow.
A feller doesn't always say
What's tuggin' at his heart,
But me and Baxter wanted you to know.

You took the path less traveled,
And penned the rustic rhyme
That captured our ambitions to the letter.
We'll carry with us always
What you prayed somebody would
'Cause, Carlos Ashley, no one says it better.

Another poem that I'm awfully proud of is "Born to This Land," which talks about passing the land from one generation to the next. Don Malone was involved in the story of that one, too.

Don invited me out to the Johnson Ranch, near Crowell, Texas. We were horseback, and I was riding with Virgil Johnson and his son, Duane, whom I had gone to college with. Duane's son, Doug, who was 14, was also with us, and he was cowboy to the core. When we would come to a gate, he would lope up ahead of us, get down from his horse, and open the gate, every time. Besides that, he really knew how to handle a horse. I was thinking, "Boy, this is something. I'm riding along here with three generations of this ranch."

I asked Virgil how long he had been on the ranch.

He said, "Well, my granddaddy settled this quarter section of land where the house is. Then my dad started helping him, but he was killed in the war. Then I helped him build it up. Now Duane and I are working together and we're working on some more acquisition." Then he just gigged his old horse and rode off. That's all he wanted to say about it.

Before we got to the chuckwagon, I had written the poem "Born to This Land" in my mind. I get a lot of response from that poem, and it's one of my favorites.

Born to This Land

I've kicked up the hidden mesquite roots and rocks
From the place where I spread out my bed.
I'm lying here under a sky full of stars
With my hands folded up 'neath my head.

Tonight, there's a terrible pain in my heart,
Like a knife—it cuts jagged and deep.
This evening, the windmiller brought me the word
That my granddaddy died in his sleep.

I saddled my grey horse and rode to a hill
Where when I was a youngster of nine,
My granddaddy said to me, "Son, this is ours—
All of it—yours, your daddy's and mine.

"Son, my granddaddy settled here after the war.
That new tank is where his house used to be.
He wanted to cowboy and live in the West,

Came to Texas from east Tennessee.

"The Longhorns were wild as the deer in them breaks.
With a long rope, he caught him a few.
With the money he made from trailin' 'em north,
Son, he proved up this homestead for you.

"The railroad got closer, they built the first fence
Where the river runs through the east side.
When I was a button, we built these corrals.
Then that winter, my granddaddy died.

"My father took over and bought up more range.
With good purebreds, he improved our stock.
It seemed that the windmills grew out of the ground.
Then the land got as hard as a rock.

"During the Dust Bowl we barely hung on.
The north wind tried to blow us away.
It seemed that the Lord took a likin' to us.
He kept turnin' up ways we could stay.

"My daddy grew older and gave me more rein.
We'd paid for most all of the land.
By the time he went on, I was running more cows,
And your daddy was my right-hand man."

His eyes got real cloudy—he took off in a trot,
And I watched as he rode out of sight.
Tho' I was a child, I knew I was special
And I'm feelin' that same way tonight.

Not many years later, my daddy was killed
On a ship in the South China Sea.
For twenty-odd years now, we've made this ranch work—
Just two cowboys, my granddad and me.

Now that he's gone, things are certain to change.
An' I reckon that's how it should be.
But five generations have called this ranch home,
And I promise it won't end with me.

'Cause I've got a little one home in a crib.
When he's old enough, he'll understand.
From the top of that hill, I'll show him his ranch
'Cause like me, he was born to this land.

Another poem that has a unique story started with my friend Ben Johnson, whom I first met while I was living in Hollywood. Ben was a great actor; he appeared in a lot of movies and won an Academy Award for his role in *The Last Picture Show*. We used to have a lot of Ben Johnson Celebrity Ropings, and they were all benefits for cystic fibrosis research. This particular time, we were in Houston and the roping was over, but I was about the last one to leave the coliseum because with my bad arm it takes me a while to saddle and unsaddle. I got to the hotel and walked in the front door. Ben was sitting on the couch in the lobby with an Indian cowboy that I knew named Joe Crow. Ben hollered at me "Red, come over here. I want Joe to tell you a story."

I walked over and sat down on the couch. Ben said, "Joe, tell Red about the time Will Rogers rode your bicycle."

I thought, what a chance to hear a great story. Joe said, "Well, when I was little, Herb McSpadden was my buddy, and I used to ride around with him in his pickup. Occasionally, he would throw my bicycle in the back of that pickup, so while he was doing whatever he needed to do, I could ride around on my bicycle.

"On this particular day, we went out to the airport to see Will Rogers, because Herb was Will's brother-in-law. Herb introduced me to Will, and then Will asked me, 'Joe, can I ride your bicycle and get the kinks out of my legs before we get on this plane?' I told him he could, so he rode my little 24-inch bicycle around that tarmac for a while.

"He came back in a minute, handed me my bicycle, and started up the ramp into the plane. Herb asked him, 'Will, where are you boys going?' and Will said, 'Herb, Wiley and I are headed to Alaska.'

"Herb said, 'Boy, there's lots of deep rivers between here and there, you be careful.'

"Will said, 'I'll make you a deal. I'll leave a good horse on this side of every one of those bad rivers.'"

I couldn't get away from them quick enough. I just saw the whole picture, the whole story. I wrote the poem "To an Old Friend," and the last line is, "If I cross the river before you get there, I'll leave a good horse on this side."

Of course, as most everyone knows, Will Rogers and his pilot Wiley Post crossed the river on that trip. Their plane crashed in Alaska, and both were killed.

To an Old Friend

I stood by the fountain as they brought him in,
A lost lonely look on his face.
I ain't never seen him in nothin' but boots.
The wheelchair shore seemed out of place.

It took him awhile to recall who I am,
But confusion turned into a grin.
It was tho' we were saddled up, ready to ride
The Hackberry Pasture again.

He laughed as he said, "I remember the time
That yeller bronc swallered his head,
And pitched you so high you turned over twice.
Me and Benny Bob swore you was dead."

He looked up at me and asked, "How is old Ben?"
I lied and said, "He's doin' fine."
No need to remind him his brother was gone.
Ben died back in '79.

For most of an hour we rode at a trot.
We branded and shaped up the steers,
Drank gallons of coffee, ate sourdough bread,
And cowboyed for fifty-one years.

I tho't he's an old man when I was a kid.
At a time when I needed a friend,
He took me to raise, taught me all that I know,
'Bout horses and cattle and men.

My daddy had died and I needed a job.
I'se big for a kid of fifteen.
They put me to work on the Four Sixes Ranch,
I'se dumb as a gourd and as green.

We's lookin' for strays in the Wichita breaks,
Was me and John Gaither and him.
I lost sight of John so I'se lookin' around,
A daydreamin' there on the rim.

Rode up on some cattle hid out in the brush.
A two-year-old steer come by me,
Throwed a nine in his tail and cut a new trail,
Right out through the salt cedar trees.

I took in behind him, agivin' it hell.
The colt I was ridin' was green.
I tho't to myself, he ain't getting away.
This roan is a running machine.

Was goin' full bore when we got to the bank.
The stream wasn't wide as my hat.
I nearly pulled up, but I tho't what the hell,
I've jumped rivers wider than that.

I bogged that old pony plumb to his gut,
Was wallerin' and thrashin' around.
He's goin' down deeper with each desperate lunge,
Me prayin' he'd find solid ground.

Then just at the moment that I heard his voice,
A rope appeared right by the roan.
"Get outta that kack and hang on to my line,
The colt'll get out on his own."

I've crossed that old river a many a time,
I've found me a bog once or twice.
But I still remember that thirty-foot rope
And this cowboy piece of advice.

"When you ride the river, son, make sure your horse
Is gentle and seasoned as well,
'Cause only the good ones will get you across.
That quicksand goes clean down to hell."

I got up to leave and he reached for my hand.
Said, "Son, I'm sure glad you dropped by.
If you see old Ben, have him saddle my horse.
I hate sittin', waitin' to die."

His voice started crackin', he swallered and said,
"I'm nearin' the end of my ride.
If I cross the river before you get there,
I'll leave a good horse on this side."

When I was a kid, I spent five summers working on my Uncle Floyd Schleusener's farm in northwestern Iowa. Floyd was raised on an Iowa farm, but while he was in the Air Force, he was stationed at the Amarillo Air Force Base and met my mother's youngest sister, Johnie. They were married, and when he got his discharge, they returned to Iowa and the farm. As soon as I was old enough, I started going up there every summer and working for Uncle Floyd.

We worked six days a week, and our days started early with Aunt Johnie fixing us a big breakfast before we headed to the barn to milk the cows, feed the hogs, gather the eggs, and then get on the tractor. I learned more in those five summers than I have all the rest of my life put together.

One lesson I learned was how to change the canvas belt on a silage wagon, but it turned out to be a lot more than that.

My uncle told me to go change that canvas belt, so I just tore into that machine, leaving parts lying around everywhere on the ground. Then when I got the canvas on the rollers, and backed off looking at all those parts, I didn't know how to put everything back together.

My uncle, of course, recognized my problem so he had me go over and look at one that was already assembled. He said, "You can see how it's supposed to look. Now, figure out how to get those parts back on."

That one lesson taught me a whole lot more than how to change the canvas belt on a silage wagon. It taught me how to put my whole life in order, how to do what I was supposed to do first.

The last summer I worked up there, which was the summer before I got polio, we were going to a field about a mile and a half from home. As we were headed down the highway, my uncle looked out his side of the pickup and, mostly to himself, said, "I'd give anything in the world if Mr. Cornwall would have those boys plow those rows straight."

I looked over on his side of the road, in the neighbor's field, and all I could see was the next stalk as we rode down the road. I looked on our side, to one of my uncle's fields, and I could see all the way through to the end of the field between every single row. I very foolishly asked, "Uncle Floyd, what difference does it make? The corn's in the ground; it's going to grow anyhow."

The color started rising just above his collar. When it got to just below the bill on his DeKalb cap, he turned to me and said, "It makes a difference to me. This is what I do. I'm a farmer, and I want to be the best I can possibly be."

I was 15 years old, but I've never forgotten that lesson. It made me realize that my destiny depended on my ability to handle the decisions that I made in my life. It was not up to my uncle, not up to my parents. It was not up to my siblings, not up to my teachers and certainly not up to the government. It was up to me to decide my destiny.

One of my uncle's neighbor's sons had a John Deere tractor, and it was one of the early models that were known as "Poppin' Johnnys" because of their distinctive exhaust sounds. I loved that old tractor and wanted to drive it so bad, but that boy wouldn't even let me kick the tire. My uncle knew how disappointed I was that Jerry wouldn't let me drive that tractor, so he bought me a book about John Deere. I read it and read it and read it, and there was one line in it that I couldn't get out of my mind. It has stayed with me all these years.

In 1856, John Deere said, "I will never put my name on a product that does not have in it the best that is in me." I try to live that way all the time. I ask myself, "Is this the best I can do?" When I finish a song or a poem, I go over every one of the lyrics with a fine-tooth comb, brush them out, and make sure it's the best I can possibly do. I think that if you truly are a good writer and you truly know your craft, it'll haunt you till you find the right line, and I love that.

Both of those stories, the one about the corn rows being straight and the one about John Deere doing his best, led me to write one of my most popular poems.

The Fence That Me and Shorty Built

We'd picked up all the fencing tools
And staples off the road.
An extra roll of "bob" wire
Was the last thing left to load.

I drew a sleeve across my face
To wipe away the dirt.
The young man who was helping me
Was tuckin' in his shirt.

I turned around to him and said,
"This fence is finally done,
With five new strands of 'bob' wire
Shinin' proudly in the sun.

"The wire is runnin' straight and tight
With every post in line.
The kinda job you're proud of,
One that stands the test of time."

The kid was not impressed at all,

He stared off into space.
Reminded me of years ago,
Another time and place.

I called myself a cowboy,
I was full of buck and bawl.
I didn't think my hands would fit
Post augers and a maul.

They sent me out with Shorty
And the ranch fence building crew.
Well, I was quite insulted
And before the day was through,

I let him know that I'm a cowboy.
"This ain't what I do.
I ain't no dadgummed nester,
I hired out to buckaroo."

He said, "We'll talk about that, son,
When we get in tonight.
Right now, you pick them augers up.
It's either that or fight."

Boy, I was diggin' post holes
Faster than a Georgia mole.
But if a rock got in my way
I simply moved the hole.

So when the cowboys set the posts,
The line went in and out.
Old Shorty's face got fiery red
And I can hear him shout.

"Nobody but a fool would build
A fence that isn't straight.

I got no use for someone who ain't
Pullin' his own weight."

I thought for sure he'd hit me;
Glad he didn't have a gun.
I looked around to find a place
Where I could duck and run.

But Shorty walked up to me
Just as calm as he could be.
Said, "Son, I need to talk to you,
Let's find ourselves a tree."

He rolled a Bull Durham cigarette
As we sat on the ground.
He took himself a puff or two
Then slowly looked around.

"Son, I ain't much on schoolin',
Didn't get too far with that.
But there's a lot of learnin'
Hidden underneath this hat.

"I got it all the hard way,
Every bump and bruise and fall.
Now some of it was easy,
But then most weren't fun a'tall.

"But one thing that I always got
From every job I've done.
Is do the best I can each day
And try to make it fun.

"I know that bustin' through them rocks
Ain't what you like to do.
By gettin' mad you've made it tough

On me and all the crew.
"Now, you hired on to cowboy
And you think you've got the stuff.
You told him you're a good hand
And the boss has called your bluff.

"So how's that gonna make you look
When he comes riding through,
And he asks me who dug the holes,
And I say it was you.

"Now we could let it go like this
And take the easy route.
But doin' things the easy way
Ain't what it's all about.

"The boss expects a job well done
From every man he's hired.
He'll let you slide by once or twice,
Then one day you'll get fired.

"If you're not proud of what you do,
You won't amount to much.
You'll bounce around from job to job
Just slightly out of touch.

"Come mornin' let's redig those holes
And get that fence in line.
And you and I will save two jobs,
Those bein' yours and mine.

"And someday you'll come ridin' through
And look across this land,
And see a fence that's laid out straight
And know you had a hand

I took my bride Gail to the offices of George W. Bush in Dallas to welcome him back home to Texas.

Gail and I were invited guests at the *White House dinner* in 2005, *honoring* the *Prince of Wales* and the Duchess of Cornwall—now known as King Charles III and Queen Camilla of the United Kingdom. (L–R): Me, Duchess Camilla, Laura Bush, Prince Charles, President Bush, and Gail Steagall. (White House Staff photo.)

"In something that's withstood the years.
Then, proud and free from guilt,
You'll smile and say, 'Boys, that's the fence
That me and Shorty built.'"

In 1983, President Reagan hosted a barbecue dinner on the White House lawn to honor the Professional Rodeo Cowboys Association during a command performance rodeo in DC. Front row (L–R): Gail Steagall, me, my late son Carl Steagall, road manager the late Jim Hammon, fiddle player the late Rick Solomon, the late President Ronald Reagan, son Steven Steagall, my late mother Ruth Robertson, bass player Dale Bruce, friend the late Dr. Dub Waltrip. Back row (L–R): rhythm guitar player and brother Danny Steagall, lead guitar Tommy Nash, steel guitar Gary Carpenter, bus driver the late Ben Stilley, drummer Lynn Massey, Mrs. Waltrip. (White House Staff photo.)

White House lawn set-up for our concert and Texas barbecue. (White House Staff photo.)

That poem is President George W. Bush's favorite, and when he was governor of Texas, he had parchment copies made for everyone on his staff. The first time I met Karl Rove, who was the president's chief of staff, he said, "I know who you are, 'The Fence That Me and Shorty Built.'"

The final time we were asked to come to the White House by President George W. Bush, we were invited to a dinner honoring Prince Charles, who, of course, is king now, and his wife Camilla. I got a call from a White House staff member who said we were on the guest list, and she wanted to know if we could make it. I assured her we could.

I felt like we were honored guests because at the dinner, I was seated next to Vice President Dick Cheney, and Gail was seated by Senator Joe Lieberman of Connecticut.

Prior to the dinner, Gail and I were in a room with the president, Prince Charles and Camilla, and just a couple of other people. We were standing there talking, and Prince Charles said to me, "I have heard all about you; you're quite a favorite of the president's. I'd like to hear some of your work sometime."

The president turned around and said, "Charlie, Shorty was a little bitty fellow, but that poem is way too long for us to stand here and listen to it now. We have to go to dinner."

Those are just a few of the things that I like to talk about as the reason for writing those particular poems. I'm proud of everything I write, because if I'm not proud of it, I don't finish it. There's a story to every one of them, but those are the most important ones.

In 1991, I was named the Official Cowboy Poet of Texas by the state legislature, a title I'll hold as long as I'm alive, and in 2006 I was named the Poet Laureate of Texas. A new poet laureate is awarded every year now, but Carlos Ashley held that title from 1948 to 1952. It makes me proud to have followed Carlos in that position.

Also in 1991, I recited "The Cowboy's Prayer" at the National Prayer Breakfast in Washington, DC. President George H. W. Bush was there, as was Reverend Billy Graham and representatives from 140 nations.

When I gave that prayer, I felt as nervous as a long-tailed cat in a room full of rocking chairs. We were in a huge ballroom in the Hilton Hotel across the river from the Capitol, and I decided I needed to get the crowd on my side before I started the prayer. I said, "Mr. President, I wish the boys in the bunkhouse could see me now. They've never seen a barn this big that wasn't full of hay.

"They did tell me," I said, "that if you needed their help, they've all got their rifle scabbards lashed to their saddles, their rifles are loaded, and they're ready to ride."

President Bush laughed and slapped his leg.

•

I've been very fortunate to have made several trips to the White House. The first one was supposed to have been in 1980, when President Jimmy Carter invited us to do a concert for the athletes who were going to the 1980 Summer Olympics in Moscow. As it turned out, President Carter decided that the United States would join sixty-five other countries and boycott the Olympics that summer in retaliation for the Soviet Union failing to comply with Carter's deadline to withdraw its troops from Afghanistan. Although we were in Washington, we didn't get to go to the White House. However, they gave the boys in the band and me sweatsuits that had U.S. Olympics printed on them.

Our second trip was in 1983, when President Ronald Reagan hosted a PRCA rodeo at the Capital Centre, which is an indoor arena in Landover, Maryland. The rodeo had a lot of the top cowboys competing, and US Secretary of Commerce Malcolm Baldrige, who was a member of the PRCA, even got in on the act. Mac competed in the team roping as a heeler; however, his header missed his loop.

The White House staff invited the band and me to have lunch in the White House dining room, and that evening we performed at a dinner following the rodeo. We set up on the South Lawn of the White House and played while the president and his guests ate what they were told was a "Western dinner" of steak, beans, and sourdough bread. The president also presented a Congressional Gold Medal to Western writer Louis L'Amour that evening, and he presented belt buckles to each of the winners of the rodeo events.

In 2002, we were in Washington, DC, to present a musical drama called *Soul of the West* at George Washington University's Lisner Auditorium. Andy Wilkinson and I wrote the play, and we presented it over a period of several years to raise money for our scholarship program. This performance in Washington was our first, and we tried to tell the story of the West through Kathleen Jo Ryan's photography and my poetry and songs.

Another good time at the George W. Bush White House with (L–R): Larry Gatlin, Gail Steagall, Janis Gatlin, President Bush, Cheryl Malone, Don Malone, and me. (White House Staff photo.)

A visit to the White House with my dear friend President George W. Bush. (L–R): Bill Zeigler, Mike Stevens, Vickie Stevens, President Bush, Jill Zeigler, Gail Steagall, and me. (White House Staff photo.)

There was a group of us there, including Larry Gatlin and his wife Janis, and the next day, we wanted to go visit the White House. Larry's son Josh worked for President George W. Bush, and he got us a special invitation to take a tour. I knew the president from when he was governor of Texas, but I didn't try to go see him. However, we were in the Lincoln Library as part of our tour when the president walked in. He was obviously in a hurry to be in a meeting, but when he saw us, he stopped and asked our tour guide how long we had been there. He didn't even know we were in the building.

The tour guide apologized and told him, "I didn't know I was supposed to tell you." She didn't know who we were, she just knew that one of her bosses had told her to take us around and show us the White House.

As the president left for his meeting, he said, "Watch for me on TV tonight. I'll be the one without the robe," so we assumed he was meeting with someone from the Middle East.

In 2005, I was the executive director of Heartland Alliance of America, and Gail and I and some friends had gone to Washington, DC, for some sightseeing after a Heartland Alliance of America meeting in Charlottesville, Virginia. We had dinner that night with Josh Gatlin, and he told the president we were in town.

The next morning, I had a call at the hotel inviting us to the White House to meet with the president. There were six of us who went: Gail and I, Jill and Bill Zeigler, and Vickie and Michael Stevens. Bill Zeigler had been a trainer for the Texas Rangers baseball team when George W. Bush was the managing general partner as well as one of the owners. Right after we cleared security, we were standing in the hallway when this door opened and the president hollered, "Hey, Zig, get in here; Red, y'all come on in."

We went with him into the Oval Office, and there were some photographers in there. He told them to get their pictures and then to get out and leave us alone. After the photographers left, he showed us all around the Oval Office and explained all the pictures and paintings. We got to spend about a half hour with him and, in fact, we made him late to a cabinet meeting. Later, when we were at the Prince Charles party, I introduced myself to Andrew Card, who was the President's Chief of Staff. He said, "I know who you are, you're the only person I've known who made the president late for a Cabinet meeting."

When we went to the Prince Charles dinner, once we got to the White House, everyone was first placed in a room where there was security with dogs checking everyone out. Gail and I didn't know anyone, and we were just standing over to the side by ourselves. Then, in walked Caroline Hunt from Fort Worth and her boyfriend, Charlie Simmons. We knew them, so we began to feel a little easier, and then here came Anne and John Marion. Anne, of course, owned the Four Sixes Ranch, and we knew her and John, so we started to relax.

As we walked from there into where the reception was going to be, there were a lot of reporters. A guy from the *Washington Post* stopped me and said, "I understand you're the Poet Laureate of Texas?" I said that I was, and he asked, "What's the Poet Laureate of Texas doing at the White House for a dinner?"

I said, "I got an invitation," and just kept walking. I thought if he was going to ask a stupid question like that, I would give him a stupid answer. The next morning, in a story in the *Washington Post*, it said, "and one of the invitees was the Poet Laureate of Texas, who said he got an invitation in the mail."

In 2022, at the Texas and Southwestern Cattle Raisers Association annual convention, I was asked to interview President Bush as part of the program at one of the general meetings. At the conclusion of the interview, I told him, "Mr. President, Gail and I truly treasure the time we were able to spend in the White House with you and Laura."

The president, who is very witty, said, "You never did bring back those saltshakers."

Just as quickly, I replied, "I guess you didn't miss the silverware."

That's the only time I was ever able to get to him. But I admire him and Laura so very much.

•

I mentioned that I was executive director of Heartland Alliance of America when we took that last trip to the White House. That position began in 2001, when Gail and I met Mike and Vickie Stevens at one of the Charles Goodnight banquets in Fort Worth. One day, Mike came out to the office and told me that he was part of a medical association called Heartland Alliance of America and that they needed an executive director. He wanted to know if that was something I would be interested in.

Heartland Alliance of America is an association of people who work together to make better deals for things like insurance policies for those involved in agriculture. It's not insurance, but rather people using their buying power as a group to make better deals for buying insurance.

Gail and I talked it over, and we decided that taking that job would give me a chance to get off the road some, not have to play a show or dance half the night, and then get up before dawn the next morning to get somewhere else. That was getting old. I took the job, and it turned out to be a good one. We built that association until it became quite sizeable and very successful.

I still played shows while I was with Heartland. I recorded some, but I didn't have to travel as much. In addition, I played lots of shows at cattlemen's conventions while I was there representing Heartland Alliance.

Having that job at that time was a big help. It made a difference in how we lived, and it allowed me to get rid of lots of things that weren't productive. Today, even though I'm no longer associated with the company, I still benefit every day from my association with my dear friends Vickie and Mike Stevens.

CHAPTER 10

FOREIGN TRAVEL

I went to twenty-three of the first twenty-five years of the Poetry Gathering in Elko. Then I skipped a few years and went back a few more, but in 1985, the first year we went, Danny and I thought we should see the famous Capriola saddle shop. We were wandering around, looking at all the tack they had there in the store, and I kept noticing this little guy following us. He was not dressed well. The cuffs on his coat were frayed, his coat didn't match his britches, his shirt didn't go with his coat or his britches, and he was carrying a brown paper bag. But every time I looked back, he was smiling at me.

Finally, I just stopped and introduced myself. He said, "My name's Joe Wilson. I'm with the National Academy for the Arts in Washington, DC. Have you ever thought about going overseas and performing for people in other parts of the world?"

I told him we had been to Germany, but that was all, and he said, "Well, we send people to entertain in other countries, and those countries send people to our country to show us how they entertain. It's part of the State Department, the United States Information Agency. We just help them find talent."

He tore off a piece of that brown paper bag and I wrote my phone number on it. I figured that was the end of it; I never thought I'd hear from him. But it wasn't two or three weeks until I got a call from the guy who was in charge of putting those trips together. He wanted to know how many people I'd bring, told me what kind of budget he had, and asked if I could live within that budget. Then he wanted all the information he could get on me and the guys in the band so we could all clear security.

And away we went to the Middle East.

We started in Jordan, and had a great time there, and then we went to Kuwait.

We were performing in a building in the back of the Jumeirah Messilah Beach Hotel in Kuwait City. On the second floor was a theater, run by a Lebanese man named Alijabar. I asked him, "Mr. Alijabar, how do we do this?"

He said, "You do a 30-minute show, take a 30-minute break, and do a 30-minute show."

I thought that was a little strange, so I asked, "Why don't we do an hour and get it over with?"

He said, "You don't understand. I cannot serve my people liquor; I can only feed them. If I feed them before the show, they go to sleep. If I feed them after the show, they get mad and go home and don't come back. I must feed them in the middle of the show."

We were there for two nights, and the second night we were out on this beautiful mosaic patio with inlaid tile. The water from the Persian Gulf was washing up on the edge, and people were taking their shoes off and dipping their toes in the water. The whole thing was breathtaking. This little fellow walked up to me, wearing a long white robe like the rest of them and with a camel hair knot on his head. He said in perfect English, "Hey, Red, my name's Fallal. What are you boys doing after the show tonight?"

I told him, "We've got to leave at 5 in the morning. We're going to Baghdad."

He said, "I told my wife we should have come last night. I have dancing girls coming to entertain you at my tent out in the desert."

I asked him, "Is that where you live?"

He said, "Oh, no, it's my ranch. It's where I keep my horses and my goats and my camels. I have people living out there who take care of it for me. I live in town. But when I was a little boy, we all lived out there."

"What kind of business are you in?"

"I'm in the family business."

"Is that oil and gas?"

"Well, some of it. I'm the king's youngest son."

"Where are your bodyguards?" I asked him. "We see sheiks and princes and kings, and they all have bodyguards."

He said, "Listen to me, Hoss. Do you think they give a shit what I do? I'm number 19. I'm never going to get to the throne." Then he added, "But I want y'all to meet my wife," and he turned and called, "Yolanda, come over here."

A statuesque woman with a long black veil and a shawl over her head walked up. Fallal said, "This is my wife; she's American Mexican."

She said, "Fallal, I've told you a hundred times, it's Mexican American." Then she turned to us. "Hi, boys, I'm from Edinburg, Texas," and she walked off.

We visited with Fallal for a couple of minutes, and I asked, "Where are the rest of your wives? You guys all have four wives apiece."

Fallal said, "Hey, listen to me. Her mom is Catholic. Can you imagine what she would do to me if I brought another woman into the house?"

We didn't get to go out to Fallal's tent in the desert and watch the dancing girls, but when we got to Baghdad, Iraq, the next day, the embassy rented a bus and drove us out to Babylon.

We spent the whole day at Babylon. It was submerged under mud 4,500 years ago, but archeologists had excavated a lot of the walls that were about 40 feet high. They were made out of mud brick roughly 14 inches square. In a 10-inch square in the middle of the wall was the news of the day, all in hieroglyphics.

While we were up on top of a ledge overlooking the river, I saw a piece of the wall lying on the ground. I picked it up and saw that it had markings on it. There was a guard standing there, so I asked him, "Can I keep this?"

In perfect English, he replied, "Sure. the next time it rains, it'll be back in the river. It's just mud."

So I put it in my fanny pack and brought it home. Now I've got a piece of the wall of Babylon at my house.

That was such an interesting trip, but we did have something funny happen. My road manager's name was Jim Hammond, and my drummer was Lynn Massey. Jim, unfortunately, was on the plane that crashed with Reba's band in 1991, so he's no longer with us. Lynn still plays drums. But the three of us were standing there watching the Bedouins bring the water buffalo down to water on the far side of the Euphrates River. Massey said, "Think about it. Three old boys from Texas standing beside the very river they floated baby Jesus down."

Hammond and I let that soak in for a minute, and then we both turned toward Massey. Hammond said, "Massey, it was Moses, and the river was the Nile."

Lynn said, "I knew that."

We all laughed about it, and "I knew that" became our byline for the rest of the trip.

Early the next morning, we were back in Baghdad and I got a call from the US Ambassador to Iraq. He said, "Red, I need you and your guys in room 126 at 8."

We got to the room early, and at 8, the ambassador walked in. He said, "Okay, boys, don't wear your hats on the streets today. Let's not look any more American than we have to because at 6 this morning the United States bombed Tripoli. We probably won't hear anything about it here, but let's not take a chance."

Tripoli is the capital of Libya, and on April 14, 1986, the United States launched air strikes against Libya in retaliation for the Libyan sponsorship of terrorism against American troops and citizens.

We went from Iraq to Syria, and while we were in the US Ambassador's residence in Damascus, we were watching NBC News. Tom Brokaw was talking about a major demonstration in front of the ambassador's residence in Damascus, Syria. He said the whole Middle East was up in arms because we had bombed Tripoli.

We looked out the window and saw some kids carrying signs that read "Down with America." They were laughing and carrying on, making sure the cameras got a shot of what their signs said, and then when they reached the end of the compound, they got in their cars and left. I realized then that it's not just other places in the world that take the news and twist it around until it's not what really happened. It happens in our country, too.

But we loved Syria. The people were so kind and nice to us. They all wanted to talk about America. One stopped us on the street and asked, "Have you ever been to Houston? My cousin has a furniture store there. Stop and see him and tell him Sharim sent you. He'll make you a good deal."

Another one said, "I have a cousin who has a restaurant in Cincinnati, Ohio. Have you ever been there?" They just loved to talk about America.

One thing that I found interesting was Syria's college of agriculture. It was a beautiful place. The students all gathered around us and one said, "We learn English, but we don't learn how to speak it. We need to be conversationalists, and we don't know how to do that." He asked us to talk to them, so they could hear us speak. We stood there for about an hour, telling them stories and talking to them about anything they wanted to hear.

We toured the Krak des Chevaliers castle, where the knights of the Crusades were defeated, and we saw the ancient city of Palmyra out in the Syrian desert. The city was just phenomenal.

I met a lot of great people in Syria and learned about a way of life that doesn't appeal to me, but it's something they treasure.

We also went to Doha, Qatar, and played in a beautiful theater. The performance was sold out. There were kids standing around the outside for two or three blocks waiting to get in, but there were only a certain number of seats. They wouldn't let anybody in that didn't have a seat. We were the first American act to be there since 1956, and we sold out that auditorium.

The manager was very impressed. He asked me, "Would you like to have some souvenir tickets?"

I said, "We'd love to," and he handed me a stack of them. The tickets said, "Come see the Red Shegali Band." Not only did he not know who we were, he didn't know how to spell my name. It was a mind-boggling trip.

In 1992, USIA (United States Information Agency) sent us to Central and South America. When we went to the Middle East, I took a six-piece Western swing band, but when we went to Central and South America, I took a five-piece cowboy band. And that worked out well because of the language. Nearly all the countries in the Americas are Spanish speaking, but in most of them, the wealthier citizens make sure their children learn English.

We started in Guatemala and spent three days there. We went to Antigua, which is the ancient city that was the original capital of Guatemala, when it was Mayan. It's pretty much now like it was then; the women still dress the same. They make their clothes with natural dyes and natural fibers.

Then we flew to Brazil. The South Region of Brazil is a recognized geographical region that includes three different states. That region is home to the largest concentration of Germans outside of Germany, the largest concentration of Italians outside of Italy, the largest concentration of Japanese outside of Japan, the largest concentration of Black Africans outside of Africa, and the largest concentration of Americans outside the United States borders.

I loved the vegetation there; the vast grasslands and the big ranches just knocked me out. However, I did not get along as well with the language in Brazil because Portuguese is the native language and it's tough to learn. Also, depending upon where you are, there are not as many people who speak English.

We went to the city of Salvador, which is in the state of Bahia in the Northeast Region. That's where the slave ships used to dock. Then we went to the Amazon River, and there's nothing like it. We were amazed at the big fish; we saw a rainbow bass bigger than a canoe. We took a boat back in through the jungle, where the Rio Negro comes into the Amazon. The Rio Negro is as black as the ace of spades because it goes through decayed vegetation and then mixes with the brown muddy water of the Amazon. There are little villages all along the Amazon River. We stopped at a rubber plantation, where they still extract rubber from the rubber trees, and we learned an awful lot. I love the southern part of Brazil. We had the best time.

Then we went to Venezuela, first to Caracas, which is the capital and largest city in Venezuela, and from there to Maracaibo, which was a big colony of American citizens who handled Venezuela's petroleum business. There is a tremendous oil reserve down there. Lake Maracaibo was full of pumpjacks and oil derricks.

From there we went to Cuidad Guyana, in the state of Bolivar. It was like a jungle paradise. The trees were full of monkeys and parrots, and those people loved us.

Our next stop was Santa Cruz, Bolivia, and it was just like being in Kingsville, Texas. People were so friendly, so kind. The mayor of Santa Cruz took us downtown in a couple of compact cars that were all dinged up. Almost all the cars are crumpled up because there aren't any stop signs. Whoever gets to the intersection first has the right of way, and they just honk constantly. The sidewalks are 30 inches higher than the street because when all trade was done with oxcarts, the merchants could back their oxcarts up and load their merchandise straight onto the cart.

When the mayor took us back to our villas, he got out a great big scrapbook, laid it on the floor, and started turning pages. There were pictures of oxcarts on those streets we had just left. I asked, "When were these taken?"

The mayor said, "1963."

I asked, "Where are the cars?"

He said, "There were no cars in Santa Cruz in 1963. We are completely isolated from the rest of South America because the Indies are the barrier between us and La Paz."

La Paz is the capital of Bolivia, and it is more than 500 miles from Santa Cruz.

We found a cowboy shop in Santa Cruz, and I think I bought eighteen rawhide reatas. I brought them home and gave most of them away as Christmas presents.

There was a big casino called Caesar's Palace in the complex where we stayed. We had little bitty bungalows, but we spent quite a bit of time in that casino.

Santa Cruz is a beautiful city, and the people there were great. I fell in love with the place.

Then we went up to Potosí, which is halfway up the mountain, about 8,500 feet. It's well known for its gold and silver mining. They take tons of precious metals out of there. We performed there in a beautiful old church.

Next, we went on up to La Paz, which is at almost 12,000 feet. It's tough to even walk at that altitude. Those people are really primitive and still live the Inca way of life. They raise 300 different varieties of potatoes in those mountains.

We also went up to Lake Titicaca, which straddles the border between Bolivia and Peru, and is 12,500 feet in altitude. There are a lot of little streams flowing into the lake, and in the afternoon, the women are all out there with their dresses full of potatoes. They put them in those little streams and they freeze. The next morning, they take them out and let them dry during the day, and then they freeze them again that night. Those potatoes last them all year that way.

When we flew home, it seemed like we flew over the Andes for hours. That's a big mountain range.

In 1993, the USIA sent us to the Far East, and our first stop was in Papua New Guinea. We landed on the seacoast and did a show in Port Moresby, which is the capital. Then we caught an old plane, I think it was a DC-3, that took us up into the highlands to Goroka.

The people all gathered around the airport to watch the plane come in. Papua New Guinea is very rural and very primitive; everyone is barefoot. There are more languages spoken on the Island of Papua New Guinea than the rest of the world put together. Every single little group of people has its own language, and they communicate by standing in the forest and yelling. If they want to go see somebody, they yell at them, and if they hear an answer, they walk that way. They loved it when we performed for them. They didn't understand what we were saying, but they loved the sound of the music.

While we were in that part of the Pacific Rim, we also did shows in Nandi and Suva, Fiji; Bangkok and Chiang Mai, in Thailand; Jakarta, Indonesia; and Seoul and Pusan, South Korea.

Those three trips with the USIA—to the Middle East, Central and South America, and the Far East—were wonderful and educational, but by the time we finished, I was ready to get back to horses and cowboys.

•

Sailing the Sea of Galilee in 2018 on a life-changing tour of the Holy Land with (front row, L–R): Bev Nuessle, Elizabeth Schumacher, Marianne Williams, Patti Toon, Sheila Ingram, Cyndi Brookshire, David Tal (our guide), and Gary Kinslow. Middle row (L–R): Mark Nuessle, Larry Williams, Larry Toon, Mike Ingram, me, Gail, Mike Rose, and Greg Brown. Back row (L–R): Peter Larsen, Caroline Larsen, Debra Kinslow, Brandy Minick, and Janet Huckabee.

I did go to the Middle East one more time. In 2018, Gail and I, and some of our friends, went with Arkansas governor Mike Huckabee and his wife Janet to Israel. Our group included Pat Martin and Dottie Worthington, Patti and Larry Toon, Sheila and Mike Ingram, Greg Brown and Brandy Minick, Deb and Gary Kinslow, Beverly and Mark Nuessle, Mike Rose and Cyndi Brookshire, and Elizabeth Schumacher. There were 319 people on the trip, but Governor Huckabee was kind enough to put all our group on the same bus while we were touring. There were, of course, some other people on that bus, too, so we made a lot of new friends, and today we refer to ourselves as the Green Bus Group.

It was a great experience. We were baptized in the Jordan River, we walked the streets we believe Jesus walked, and we stood in places where he preached sermons. It was a life-changing experience. We learned an awfully lot about the Israeli people, how they live, what motivates them, and what their struggles are to stay alive as a society.

Gail and I have traveled the world with lots of very special friends, including Cheryle and Tom Elliott, Suzie and Tim Cox, Dolores and Dick McHargue, Brenda and Johnny Jones, Jana and Johnny Trotter, Dr. Eleanor Green and Dr. Jim Heird, Holly and Rob Farrell, Lynne and Cliff Teinert, Cherokee and

Jim Charlesworth, Janie and Bruce Greene, Shirley and Clarence Ritchie, and Vickie and Mike Stevens, among many others. On one memorable trip involving a cruise on the Danube River, one of my longtime, most loyal fans, who has become a special friend through these forty-plus years, met our flight in Frankfurt with a bus to drive our group of six to the port in Nuremburg for our departure on the ship. Achim Gutbrod and his darling wife Monika were there to make sure that our group made our connection. I will always consider that a true example of loyalty and friendship, coming to our rescue in a foreign country!

CHAPTER 11

TEXAS RANCH INFLUENCES

One evening in early spring 1977, I was in Frisco, Texas, having dinner at the home of Anne and B. F. Phillips Jr. Anne was the daughter of Anne Burnett Tandy and the great-granddaughter of S. B. "Burk" Burnett, who established the famous Four Sixes Ranches. Anne had inherited the Four Sixes from her mother. Anne and B. F. were later divorced, but they were married at that time. During dinner, B. F. looked at me and said, "We're going to the Sixes for the spring roundup next week. Why don't you go with us?"

I couldn't say yes fast enough. The following week I rode with them down to Guthrie, Texas, where the Four Sixes was headquartered. All the way down there, I was dreaming of staying at the chuckwagon, sleeping in a tepee, and riding with the cowboys, something I had wanted to do since I was a child growing up in Sanford, watching those cowboys on the Sanford Ranch. However, when we got there, I found that they didn't put the wagon out anymore, as they had previously for years and years. That year, for the first time, instead of moving the wagon from pasture to pasture, it was staked down in the Mulberry Pasture just north of the headquarters. All the cowboys had breakfast there and came back there for dinner, but they stayed at their homes or in the bunkhouse at night and traveled from pasture to pasture in pickups and trailers. The single

Horseback on the 6666 Ranch with (L–R) longtime ranch manager, the late J. J. Gibson, the late Bill Owen, and me.

I'm in the middle of two of my best friends—Greg Brown (left) and the late Bill Owen (right).

Me and my forever pal and jokester, the famous cowboy artist, the late Bill Owen.

Riding the range with a couple of punchers, including cowboy artists the late Bill Owen (center) and the late Joe Beeler (second from right). I'm mounted well on my old pal Apollo (right).

boys had supper at the wagon, but all the married cowboys returned to their homes and had supper with their families.

It broke my heart, but I made the best of it. Ranch general manager J. J. Gibson caught me a big dun horse named Tonk to ride, and I did get to live out the rest of my dream, riding with the cowboys and helping them work cattle.

We came back into Fort Worth in time for me to play at the Copenhagen/Skoal Calf Roping Championship that following weekend, and while the band was setting up in the arena at the Cowtown Coliseum in the Fort Worth Stockyards, I sat down on a drum case and wrote the song "Horses and Wars." It's about the end of an era and has a couple of lines in it that go like this: "Now the cow camp is empty, the land's full of fences. Cowboys feed hay in a truck. The chuckwagon stands in a museum in Kansas, rottin' and gatherin' dust."

That song came to be one of the most important of my career and influenced a lot of people, especially the Cowboy Artists of America, who, like me, are trying to leave a picture of cowboy life for those yet to come. Of course, the song came from the time I had spent on the Four Sixes Ranch just a few days before.

That experience really affected me. I went back to the Sixes twenty-nine of the next thirty years for spring works, and J. J. treated me like royalty. He taught me how to do things from a cowboy's standpoint. I got to watch how those guys worked, what kind of people they were, how much respect they paid to the brand. When I started writing poetry and cowboy songs, I drew on the experiences that I had with those cowboys. It gave me a real sense of who the cowboy was and what I needed to preserve for future generations in my poetry and songs.

After Anne and B. F. were divorced, she married John Marion. She was as dear a friend as I'll ever have in my life. We lost Anne in 2020, but I have the highest respect for her. She represents a special chapter that made a difference in my world.

J. J. Gibson was a giant, in my estimation, and I think the world of his son, Mike, who succeeded him as general manager. Joe Leathers, today's general manager, is as fine a gentleman, and as good a horseman and cattleman, as ever walked the face of this earth. I'm a very blessed boy to have been able to work with all those men.

For almost fifty years, I have been honored to ride horses that were bred and raised on the Four Sixes Ranch. I made lots of memories and covered lots of miles on the finest cow horses on the planet, like Apollo, Sonny Boy, Junior, and Six Shooter, just to name a few.

•

Back in the mid-1990s, I had a group of friends who, like me, loved the ranching lifestyle and deep down wondered if they could have lived that lifestyle. We decided to find out.

I made arrangements with the JA Ranch in the Texas Panhandle for a group of us to bring our horses and spend a week camped with the ranch cowboys during spring works: get up when they did every morning, catch our horses and saddle them, and be ready to trot out of camp before the sun came up in the east.

The JA is one of the oldest and most historic ranches in the state. It was founded in 1876 by famous trail driver Charles Goodnight and his partner John Adair, and it lies in the bottom of Palo Duro Canyon, the second largest canyon in the United States. The terrain is brushy and rough, with one canyon after another, and in the bottom lies the Prairie Dog Town Fork of the Red River, which a few miles downstream becomes the border between Texas and Oklahoma. At one time, the ranch encompassed 1,335,000 acres, but through the years it has been reduced to approximately 200,000 acres. That's still more than 300 square miles. The ranch today is owned by Mrs. Adair's great-granddaughter, Ninia Ritchie, and Ninia's son, Andrew Bivins.

Our ranch manager at the time, Bobby Johnston, is a great cook, so I got him to haul my chuckwagon to the ranch and cook for us. JA ranch foreman Billy Hollowell designated where we would camp, and on the day we arrived, we set up the wagon and everyone set up their tepees. No plastic or nylon tents were allowed, only canvas tepees, and canvas cowboy bedrolls were encouraged. All the trucks and trailers were parked elsewhere on the ranch. Only one pickup was allowed nearby in case of an emergency. Our only transportation was horseback.

The first night we were there, the ranch's wagon boss, Carroll Jack Lewis, explained what was going to happen. He said that the next morning, we would trot out of camp in a long line and periodically he would drop each one of us off at a different spot. He didn't say that we would be trotting twenty-five miles, but we did. He said that after we were all dropped off, at a signal from him, we would ride forward, combing our way through the brush, pushing in front of us any cattle we saw, toward a set of pens, where we would brand the calves.

He said there would be times we would not see another cowboy anywhere, and that it would be very easy to get lost. If anyone got lost, they should ride to the highest, closest hill and sit down. Somebody would find them. He

Dragging calves to the fire at the JA Ranch in 2009.

emphasized that everyone should stay in the pasture where they were dropped off, and to not cross a fence. He said, "If you cross a fence and get in another pasture, we may not find you for three or four weeks, and you won't be in very good shape when we do."

That canyon is vast, and when you get down on that second level, there are a lot of washouts and every one of them looks like the next one. We had several guys get disoriented and lose track of where they were, but they sat down under a tree and we found them.

When we got to the ranch, we belonged to the wagon boss. I may have gotten the guys there, but they didn't belong to me. They belonged to the wagon boss, and he treated us just like we were day workers. Each day, when we got the cattle penned, he assigned every one of us a job. Some started out dragging calves to the fire and some started out flanking, while others vaccinated, ear marked, or branded. Some of the guys were good ropers in an arena, but heeling a calf and dragging it to the branding fire is a completely different art form. Everyone learned so many things about ranch life, and they all enjoyed it.

The first year, there were only seven of us, and we worked cattle for five days, long trotting about twenty-five miles a day. On the last day—we were leaving the next morning—we decided we would spend the night at the ranch bunkhouse. That evening, we were sitting on the porch of the bunkhouse, and

I told the guys, "If we do this again, I need to know what you liked and what you didn't like."

Dick DeGuerin said, "Don't change a thing. I loved every minute of it."

Butch Robinson said, "It's the greatest experience of my life. Don't do anything different."

Mickey Pillow, who has since passed away but was with us on that first trip, said, "Well, there's two things I want to know. First of all, when we get ready to go somewhere, I want to know how far it is. I don't want to hear, 'It's just right over yonder.' The other thing I want to know is what time we're leaving."

Wagon boss Carroll Jack Lewis, all week long, had been pretty matter of fact about what we needed to do. He said, "Well, Mickey, I don't know how far it is over there. It might be one mile, two miles, six miles, I don't know, but it's just right over yonder. And we've got to trot because we'll never get there in a walk. So we just go to work. But as far as the time we're leaving, if you see this screen door hit my butt, my horse is already saddled."

Mickey never came back for spring works.

We ended up doing that for twenty years. A few guys were there every year, while others rotated in and out, and we got to where we had as many as twenty guys.

When Charles Goodnight was running the JA Ranch, he hired some hunters to clean the buffalo out of the canyon in order to save the grass for his cattle. Mrs. Goodnight sent some of the ranch cowboys to gather some of the buffalo calves that were left and bring them back to the ranch headquarters. She raised those calves, which ended up being all that was left of what was known as the Panhandle herd that at one time numbered in the millions. The descendants of those buffalo calves continued to live on the ranch for the next hundred years or so.

On one of our trips to the JA, on one particular day, we were pushing about 250 cows and calves down a fence row. Mike Rose was riding beside me, and he said, "You know, we've been coming here several years now, and we've never seen the buffalo. I don't believe there are any."

Mike had no more than gotten those words out of his mouth when here the buffalo came, stampeding over the hill. They ran right through the fence, through the middle of the cattle, knocking calves in the air, knocking cows down. They disappeared over the next hill and were gone, and no one said a word. Everyone was shocked. In a little bit, here they came back. You could almost feel the ground shaking when they ran. There weren't but about sixty of them, but it seemed like 6,000.

Ninia finally decided the buffalo needed to leave the ranch, and she gave them to the state of Texas, which moved them to Caprock Canyons State Park. There they graze the pastures in the bottom of that canyon just like they did for thousands of years. Today, there are probably only one or two of those original animals that were on the JA left, but they are the purest bison DNA left on the plains. Mrs. Goodnight saved them, and Ninia preserved them for the people of Texas.

Some years when we were there, the weather was good; other years it was bad. One year it rained 11 inches; another year, it snowed. When we got up the next morning there was ice and snow all over the tepees. By midmorning, it had kinda melted off, so we saddled up and went to work. However, I looked up and about half our crew was gone. They had all of that they could handle. They weren't as tough as they wanted to be.

But there was always something. Either the wind got up to seventy miles an hour or it was colder than the dickens. One year, we stayed at the Battle Creek Pens, and it was 16 degrees three nights in a row. That's cold in a cowboy tepee. But we got up, fed our horses, saddled, and rode out of there.

It was a wonderful experience, and those of us who stayed loved it. Every time a group of us get together, we laugh and carry on and talk about our experiences at the JA.

For me, it was even more. Those times I was able to spend at the ranch did a couple of things for me. First, they let me live out my dreams, and second, they gave me material to write about in an authentic manner, which is important to me. I could write about things that I had actually seen, and I was able to write songs and poems about some of the stories the cowboys told around the fire in the evening. I owe a great deal of gratitude to Miss Ninia Ritchie, her son Andrew Bivins, ranch manager Jay O'Brien and all the cowboys I had an opportunity to ride with. That includes Billy Hollowell; Randall Gates, who succeeded Billy as foreman; and Rhett Cauble, who succeeded Carroll Jack as wagon boss. It was the chance of a lifetime, and I will forever be grateful.

Another time, some friends and I were on a trail ride on the Lambshead Ranch, which is near Albany, Texas. Three friends from Houston came up—Steve Pierce, Mike Rose, and Mike Powers—and there was a man who came with them that I didn't know. His name was Albert Grimaldi. We rode for five

Crossing the Brazos River on my old pony, Badger.

days, setting up camp with our tepees each evening and tearing down every morning so we could move to another site. We would throw our tepees and bedrolls in the chuckwagon so they would be at our new camp. One evening, we were camped alongside the Clear Fork of the Brazos River, and Albert and I were talking at the campfire. He asked me, "Red, how long has your family been in Texas?"

I said, "Since 1870, for five generations. Both sides of my family came from Tennessee after the War of Northern Aggression. How about you?"

He said, "I live in the same house my family has lived in for 900 years."

I was speechless. After a little bit, I told Mike Rose, "Albert told me that he lives in the same house his family has lived in for 900 years."

Mike asked, "Don't you know who that is, Red?"

"Yeah," I answered, "it's Albert Grimaldi."

Mike said, "He's the Prince of Monaco."

Visiting my friend Prince Albert at his palace in Monaco.

I felt so stupid. I was knocked for a loop. I didn't see the Prince of Monaco. All I saw was this nice guy named Albert Grimaldi who was dressed just like the rest of us and rolled his own bed every morning, fed his own horse, and set up his own tepee every evening. We became good friends on that ride.

Later, in a *National Geographic* magazine article, a reporter asked him, "Where would you like to be more than anywhere else in the world?"

Albert said, "I would like to be in West Texas riding with my cowboy friends."

Where we were riding was only a few miles from the remains of old Fort Griffin, which had been constructed during the Indian wars as protection for the settlers in the area. Fort Griffin was abandoned in 1881 and today is a state historical site. On one of the days we were riding, Cliff Teinert and I were out in front, when suddenly a troop of cavalry, wearing uniforms and carrying weapons from about 1875, came out of the brush. They were riding in formation, and when they got close to us, the officer in charge called for them to halt. He then rode up to me, saluted, and said, "Mr. Steagall, we've come to lead your group to the fort." He saluted again, turned his horse, rode back through the troop, and took his place at the head of the column.

We followed them, and no one said a word until we got way on up the hill. It was one of the most dramatic things I've ever seen. I didn't know it was going to happen; Cliff had set it up. But we were all overwhelmed.

Albert Grimaldi is an American—he has dual citizenship—and for his fiftieth birthday, he wanted to have visited every state in America. He called and asked if I would take him to the National Cowboy Hall of Fame. Gail and I met him in Oklahoma City and showed him around the whole museum. When he started to leave, he said, "If you ever get a chance to come over to my part of the world, I'd like to host you in my country."

Not too much later, Gail and I, and Lynne and Cliff Teinert, went to Monaco, and while we were there, we had breakfast with Albert in the palace garden. Then he had to show us his man cave. There were big pictures of naked women all the way around it, and he said, "Girls, I hope this doesn't embarrass you, but the women in my house don't ever get to come in here."

Before we went to Europe, Cliff and I had Stuart Williamson of Taos, New Mexico, make Albert a pair of beautiful spurs and we had Gary Dunshee of Big Bend Saddlery in Alpine, Texas, make the spur leathers. Albert loved them. He is a very dear friend. We hear from him every once in a while, and always at Christmas.

CHAPTER 12

COMRADERIES

In 1970, I went to the Bob Marshall Wilderness in northwestern Montana with my friend Dave Burgess to hunt grizzly bear and elk. I had drawn a grizzly bear tag, and that was the first time in twenty-two years that a grizzly bear tag had been drawn in that particular camp with that outfitter. That was a big deal, and I killed a bear. However, it did something to me. That was the last large animal I've ever killed. After we skinned that bear out and I saw that naked body lying in that snowbank, it kinda got to me.

Dave killed an elk on that trip, and I helped him get it back to camp. I would do that again tomorrow. I've been hunting a jillion times since then with friends, and I've helped them field dress their game and get it back to our camp. I just decided I would not kill any more large animals.

But way more important than my killing that grizzly bear on that trip was the fact that I met a man named Fred Fellows. Fred was a cowboy and a cowboy artist who lived in Bigfork, Montana. For some reason, he and I hit it off immediately, and we became like brothers. We talked all the time. The year before, he had been asked to join Cowboy Artists of America, which is a group of artists who are committed to making quality and authentic art that portrays the cowboy West. The group was only four years old when the members asked Fred to join them. Today, there are thirty-four members of the CA who, through the years, have set the standard for contemporary Western realism. They are the best and most authentic Western artists in the world.

Fred and I stayed in touch and visited each other as often as we could. A few years later, I went to one of the Cowboy Artists shows in Kansas City. Fred was there, and he invited me to attend one of the group's trail rides, which they have every year at some ranch in the West. The trail rides are like an annual meeting, and that is when the members conduct the group's business. Those rides also promote comradery among the members and are looked forward to every year.

The first one I attended was in 1976 on a ranch at Saddlestring, Wyoming, near Buffalo. I've missed only two trail rides since then. One was in Hawaii, which I didn't get to attend because of a scheduling conflict, and the other one was at the Kokernot 06 Ranch in far West Texas. At that time, I was recovering from COVID-19 and didn't have the strength to make the trip.

At the 1983 trail ride, which was at Vermejo Park in Northern New Mexico, I had brought my horse and thrown him in with the others in preparation for a ride the next day. That night, we were all sitting around the fire at our camp, just talking, and Joe Beeler, who was one of the CA founders, said, "I think we need to make Red an honorary member."

Frank Polk, who stuttered badly, said, "H-h-hell, I th-th-thought he was. He's b-b-been here forever."

They made me an honorary member that night, and those guys have become my family and their families have become our families. I treasure every single one of them. Gail and I have had some of the most wonderful experiences with that group of men and their wives.

Nearly all the guys who were at that camp at Vermejo Park that night are gone. But new guys have come along, some great artists, and I admire their work just as much as I do that of the older guys. They are all a big part of my life. Their paintings hang on my walls, and their sculptures are on pedestals in my office, in my living room, and in the bedrooms of my house.

•

Another group that I'm very close to is what we now call Red's Rangers.

In 2009, four couples who were close friends—Holly and Rob Farrell, Pam and Roy Gene Evans, Mary and Randy Upshaw, and Teresa and Luther King—came over to our house for dinner. They knew that I was a historian, so they started asking me questions about the great Comanche chief Quanah

L–R: Bill Heard, Mike Stevens, me, Mike Ingram, and Martin Harrison living it up on one of our Red's Ranger trips.

Parker, whose mother had been a white captive who had been adopted into the Comanche tribe. They wanted to know where all he had been and what all he did. After a little bit I suggested that we rent a bus and drive up to Cache, Oklahoma, where Quanah had lived with his five wives after he had left the warpath and, for the most part, adopted the white man's ways.

That was the beginning of our annual history tour, which today includes thirty-five men who enjoy getting together, having a good time, and studying historical sites. They have named our group Red's Rangers, and we've been

Red's Rangers ride again. (L–R): Rob Farrell, Randy Upshaw, Bruce Greene, Mike Richards, Tony Spears, Cliff Teinert, me, Larry Work, Roy Gene Evans, Gerald Nobles, Gary Kinslow, Tio Kleberg, and Jay Evans.

A few of Red's Rangers touring Mount Rushmore. (L–R): Cliff Teinert, me, Roy Gene Evans, Randy Upshaw, Mike Richards, Greg Brown, Luther King, Jim Brosche, and Rob Farrell.

everywhere. We went to the Texas Panhandle to follow the trail of Quanah Parker, and then we went all over the state exploring the stories of the birth of the Republic of Texas. We went on a forts tour, where we visited several of the old forts that have been restored; we went to Calgary, Alberta, Canada, for the rodeo; and we've been to Northern California to the wine country. We took a trip to North and South Dakota, we went to Wyoming and Montana, and we traveled to Charleston, South Carolina.

L–R: Special friend, major Arizona real estate developer Mike Ingram, world-famous vocalist Steve Amerson, and me.

We've become an extremely close group of guys, and I wouldn't trade anything in the world for that group. It's a big part of my world.

There are some other groups that I'm also very close to and that mean a tremendous amount to me. I found out about the first one in 1982 when I met a

L–R: Cowboy artist Bruce Greene, entrepreneur Gary Kinslow, me, and real estate tycoon Larry Toon—some of my best friends—on a train trip to Canada.

man named Bruce Weaver who owned a Western-wear store in Houston called Way Out West. I played a show for Bruce, and he urged me to join a group that he belonged to called Tejas Vaqueros. He told me it was a group of men who met each year on a ranch in the Texas Hill Country, and that they rode horses, roped, and just generally enjoyed each other's company.

I went as a guest that year, and then I was invited to join. I went the next year as a Maverick, which is what they call first-year members, and I've been a member

L–R: Gary Kinslow, me, Bruce Greene, and Larry Toon on the Rocky Mountaineer traveling across Canada.

Traveling the Rocky Mountaineer trail with (L–R): Bruce Greene, Janie Greene, Patti Toon, Larry Toon, me, Gail, Debra Kinslow, and Gary Kinslow.

L–R: Me, Tony Spears, Tio Kleberg, and Cliff Teinert somewhere between Banff and Lake Louise, Canada.

ever since. Tejas Vaqueros became a very important part of my world. My circle of friends expanded dramatically, and I talk to some of those guys almost weekly.

Before Mother passed away, she developed a tumor in her eye; the doctor was going to remove the eye. Because of Tejas Vaqueros, I had gotten to know Dr.

Me and Gail at the Husky Homestead, Denali Park, Alaska, 2023.

Red Duke, who was a trauma surgeon at Memorial Hermann-Texas Medical Center in Houston. I called Red and he put me in touch with the people at Texas Southwestern Medical Center. They saved Mother's eye.

In 1988, two of my Tejas Vaqueros friends, Don Barnes and Park Meyers, invited me to attend the Los Rancheros Visitadores ride in California as an

A group of my Ranchero friends including the late President Ronald Reagan (second from left), the late Gene Autry (second from right), and my dear friend, the late Don Edwards (far right).

Monte Montana (left) and me at Rancheros Visitadores in Santa Ynez, California.

entertainer. Los Rancheros Visitadores is a group similar to Tejas Vaqueros, and although their gathering is in California, they have members from all over the United States. In 1992, Don Barnes, Gilbert Aguirre, and Tony Moiso sponsored me as a Maverick in Rancheros Visitadores and I became a member.

When I began to have trouble with my kidneys, Johnny Trotter and his wife, Jana, from Hereford, Texas, got me an appointment with Dr. Inderbir Gill at the USC Institute of Urology in Los Angeles. Dr. Gill saved my kidneys. Several of my Rancheros Visitadores friends are on the board of directors of the USC Institute of Urology and they continue to grease the skids at that facility for Gail and me.

The fifth group to which I belong is called Portola Riders, which, like Tejas Vaqueros and Los Rancheros Visitadores, is a group of men who meet on a ranch each year. The Portola Riders gather at the Rancho Mission Viejo in Orange County, California. Rancho Mission Viejo was established in 1845. The owner today is Tony Moiso, who is a descendant of the man who bought the ranch in 1862, and Tony and his friend Gilbert Aguirre host the Portola Riders each year. Gilbert and Tony are two of the men who sponsored me in Rancheros Visitadores and both are very close friends.

A sixth ride—one that is close to home—is called the Cowboy Spring Gathering, which began in 1986 to commemorate the Texas Sesquicentennial. Rob Farrell and a group of friends wanted to remember and honor the sacrifices of our forebears. It began on the Colorado River in Central Texas and was later moved to Erath County, then to Palo Pinto County and now to Bosque County. It started out as a father and son ride where everyone would bring their sons and grandsons, and we would have about a hundred people. Lots of the youngsters were inner city kids who never had a chance to touch a horse or even see one up close or do anything outdoors like we were doing. We would rope and ride, and some of them became pretty doggone good cowboys as they grew older.

We had entertainment, things like washer pitching and all kinds of equine events like cattle sorting, pasture roping, and trail rides.

One year that I remember especially was back before John Gaither died. John was a cowboy with whom I had ridden lots of miles at the Four Sixes for years, and we all just idolized him. He was a great cowboy, and we paid attention to how he did things because it was the right way. On this particular year, we were having a pasture roping, and Bill Heard and I were teamed with John. John was going to head and I was going to heel, and Bill was our mugger. His job was to take the ropes and sale tag off the steer and then we would all beat it back to the finish line.

Bill and I kinda stayed out of the way until John headed the steer and then, by a miracle, I roped two heels. We stretched the steer out while Bill jumped off his horse and took our ropes and the tag off. We won that roping. Bill and I have been bragging about it for years because there were two world champion ropers in that contest that morning, and we beat them.

Today, things have changed out on the Brazos, and we have the Spring Gathering at Marc Myers's Old Sundown Ranch outside of Meridian, Texas. It's still the same group of guys, and now we're seeing grandsons bringing their sons. It's a multigenerational thing, and we're proud to hopefully bring some of the values of the cowboy way of life to a group of young people who otherwise would have known very little about it. They become part of it and they love it, and we hope they'll raise their sons that way.

The comradery that has developed at the Cowboy Spring Gathering is unparalleled, and every year it adds another dimension to our lives. It's just like brothers, it's like a fraternity and we're all very proud to be a part of it. A group that evolved from my friendship with some of the men is our Bible study group that meets on Wednesday mornings on Zoom. Those men include our spiritual leader, Dudley Hall, along with Rob Farrell, Ron Hall, Bill Benton, Harold Wilson, Randy Upshaw, Mike Richards, Bill Heard, Roy Gene Evans, Alan Friedman, and Ron Goode.

As it turns out, it's not just the men who get together. In 2001, Gail decided she wanted to have a trail ride, but she didn't want any horses along. She leads a group of up to thirty-five women friends to a spa they love in Mexico. For a week they're being pampered, fluffed, and buffed. Gail says that this is where she gets her batteries recharged every year. Some years they go twice. I think it just depends upon how they're feeling as to when they go. But they have a good time.

Occasionally, Gail and I reminisce about how fortunate we are to have so many great friends from so many different places. All these friends have made our lives wonderful.

CHAPTER 13

RED STEAGALL COWBOY GATHERING AND WESTERN SWING FESTIVAL

In 1991, two Tarrant County AgriLife Extension agents, Jalyn Burkett and John South, came up with the idea of putting on a cowboy gathering at the Stockyards in Fort Worth. Cowboy gatherings were becoming a big thing in certain areas of the West, and Fort Worth just seemed to be a natural place to hold one. They asked if I would join them at the first meeting, which we held in the boardroom at the top of the Cowtown Coliseum in the Stockyards.

Also meeting with us was Don Edwards, a local singer whom everyone knew and loved, and who was my favorite cowboy balladeer. Don was our star attraction until his health prevented him from participating as an entertainer. Don died in 2022.

L–R: Jimbo Calhoun, me, and Steve Murrin, longtime partners in the Red Steagall Cowboy Gathering. Missing in this photo is our other partner, the late Hub Baker.

At that first meeting, we decided to add the words "Western swing festival" to the title of the event because Fort Worth was the birthplace of Western swing, going clear back to Milton Brown and his Musical Brownies and Bob Wills and the Texas Playboys. Milton Brown and Bob Wills are held to be the cofounders of Western swing. Then, Jalyn and John asked if I would add my name to the event, and I readily agreed. It became the Red Steagall Cowboy Gathering and Western Swing Festival.

Our goal was to raise money for scholarships, and we started in a big way. We had a chuckwagon camp on the lawns of both the Exchange Building and Cowtown Coliseum, and there was lots of cowboy music and poetry with presentations by professionals and children. There was a fiddle contest, and we had a Western swing festival, with dances on Friday and Saturday nights. There was also a ranch rodeo, which showed the skills of the ranch cowboy. This rodeo didn't have bull riding or bulldogging, just events that originated on the ranch, like roping, bronc riding, and branding.

We also had a cowboy trappings and trade show that featured items for sale that represented the West. The trade show was juried, and any booths that included items that weren't indicative of the West were rejected.

That first year, it rained 11 inches. The rain kept putting out the chuckwagons' cookfires, but the show went on and when it was over, we had broken even on our finances. The next year, we came back and did it again, and that time we were able to make enough money to award our first scholarships.

After three years of the event, Jalyn and John both retired from the extension service and turned the gathering over to me. I recruited three friends: Steve Murrin, who at that time owned numerous Fort Worth Stockyards businesses—rancher Jimbo Calhoun; and Hub Baker, who was general manager of the Cowtown Coliseum—and we went to work.

We kept all the events we had, but we added a wagon train that originates in Jacksboro, which is sixty miles away, and ends up in the Stockyards, and we added a team roping. In 2023, counting the whole weekend of the event, there were more than 40,000 people roaming around the Stockyards.

In 2000, Gail and I joined with a group of friends and founded the Cowboy Heritage Association of Fort Worth, which has become our scholarship foundation. The success of our scholarships has been tremendous. We have helped numerous single mothers further their education, get jobs, and get off welfare. Many of those entered the computer field, while one became an X-ray technician and one became an airline mechanic. We also give scholarships to the students who win the children's fiddle contest, the children's poetry contest, and the children's cookoff at the Gathering, and we give scholarships to children of working ranch families.

Our first poetry contest scholarship winner came from the east side of Fort Worth. A young girl told us that she had never been any further west than the city limits of Fort Worth, but she did some research in the school library and wrote a beautiful poem about Black cowboys. She was so impressed that people she identified with had something to do with the settlement of North Texas. She became the first person in her family to graduate from high school, and she went on to get a degree in electrical engineering from Rice University.

We have had two recipients, both women, who graduated from Harvard Law School, and the general manager of the world-famous Pitchfork Ranch, when he was a student, was able to go through the Texas Christian University Ranch Management Program with our help. Other ranch-raised boys who earned scholarships either have or have had management positions at the Bell Ranch in New Mexico and the Four Sixes Ranch in Texas.

To date, we've awarded more than $2 million in scholarships to deserving young people throughout Texas, and they've gone to all kinds of schools. We

On the town with some of our best friends. (L–R): Greg Brown, Brandy Minick, Gail, and me.

don't care where they go to school, just so they go. Our largest benefactor for most of these years has been Andrea "Tudy" Harkins, representing her mother's foundation. Without her we could never have been able to serve this number of students.

Our scholarships have been a very important thing to me. Often, all a person needs is a leg up. If they have a desire to go ahead and do something with themselves, they will perceive the light at the end of the tunnel not as an oncoming train but as a bright opportunity.

Each year, I get horseback and lead the wagon train into the Stockyards. In 2019, on the 29th anniversary of the Gathering, a life-size bronze statue of me horseback leading the chuckwagons into the historic Fort Worth Stockyards was dedicated on the lawn of the Cowtown Coliseum. The bronze was created by my very good friend Bruce Greene, whom I had gotten to know through my association with the Cowboy Artists of America. Over the last few years, Bruce and I have become as close as brothers, and there are no words to express my appreciation to him and my friends who commissioned the bronze: Deb and Gary Kinslow, Jana and Johnny Trotter, Sheila and Mike Ingram, and Greg Brown and Brandy Minick.

This all began as a surprise to me, when on my 80th birthday, Gail took me to dinner at Shady Oaks Country Club in Fort Worth. At the table were the

Kinslows, the Trotters, the Ingrams, and Greg and Brandy. Shortly after dinner, Janie and Bruce Greene joined us, and Bruce showed me a sketch of the bronze he was working on, which was, of course, the bronze of me sitting on my horse Apollo, a good Four Sixes mount, welcoming people to the Stockyards. I was so overwhelmed that evening that I was speechless. I'm so deeply honored because to have a bronze in your honor, that's going to stand there as long as the elements will allow it to, is pretty mind-boggling. I'm still overwhelmed every time I'm in the Stockyards and see the bronze.

But that bronze being there on the lawn of the Cowtown Coliseum didn't just magically materialize. My friend Hub Baker, who at the time was manager of the Cowtown Coliseum, walked the process through city government and made it happen.

The year 2022 marked the 32nd anniversary of the Red Steagall Cowboy Gathering and Western Swing Festival, and that year I turned management of it over to the American Paint Horse Association (APHA). David Dellin is executive vice president of APHA, and the association offices are in Mule Alley in the Stockyards. Even though I relinquished management, I am still involved.

CHAPTER 14

MEDIA LIFE

In 1992, a friend named Mac Churchill asked me to speak to the Rotary Club in Fort Worth. Mac owned a car dealership in Fort Worth. When the Rotary Club meeting was over, he called his advertising agency, which was owned by Stuart Balcom, and asked Stuart to see if I would do a poem on a three-minute show every morning, five days a week, on WBAP Radio in Fort Worth. Mac said he would sponsor the show.

On a three-minute show, you actually have only two minutes of content time, because you need a 60-second commercial to pay for the show. I told Stuart I didn't have any two-minute poems, so Mac asked what it would take. I told him at least a half hour, and Mac said, "Let's do a demo and we'll see if we can get someone to carry the show on a weekly basis. I'll still sponsor it."

I drove into Jim Hodges's studio in Fort Worth and cut a 30-minute demo of a radio show called *Cowboy Corner*. It turned out pretty good, and I sent it to my friend Michael Oatman at KFDI Radio in Wichita, Kansas. He and Mike Lynch owned twenty-two stations at the time. Michael Oatman called me and said, "Red, I love this show. There's a niche market for it. If you'll make it an hour show, I'll put it on every single radio station I've got."

The program director at WBAP said the same thing: he wanted an hour show. So Stuart, Mac, and I thought we should pursue this idea. I got with Bob and Nan Kingsley, whom I had met while I was in Hollywood—Bob was the one who urged me to join the Academy of Country and Western Music—and we put together an hour show.

Nan was very active in radio advertising, and she secured us a good sponsor. I was doing some projects for Cabin Fever Videos, and I got them to take a spot. We went on the air with 164 radio stations.

We were on the air and doing well, but we still needed some help, so we went to the bank and borrowed $150,000. We paid that loan off in one year.

Later, Mac decided he wanted out of the project, so Stuart and I bought him out; we decided to give the Kingsleys a third of the show because Nan was providing nearly all the ads for us. Then Stuart got a job as the advertising agent for Justin Boot Company, and he suggested they buy a spot. We all realized that probably wasn't right, due to a conflict of interest on Stuart's part, so Nan and Bob, and Gail and I, bought Stuart out.

The show has been going thirty-one years now, and today, we're on 140 to 145 stations in thirty-four states—we have never had fewer than 120 stations. Bob passed away in 2019, but Gail, Nan, and I own 100 percent of the show.

We have a very loyal listening audience. I record some of the shows on the road and some in the studio in my office. We play cowboy music, offer a song of inspiration, and I interview people who have a vested interest in the preservation and perpetuation of the Western way of life. I'm very proud of *Cowboy Corner*. The show and its audience have done more than just about anything else to keep my name alive in the world of entertainment.

Around 2008, I decided I wanted to take that same format and adapt it to television. I wanted to do a cowboy variety show with poets, singers, and chuckwagon cooks—all the things that were incidental to the cowboy way of life. My very dear friend Greg Brown at that time owned *Cowboys & Indians* magazine, where I have a dedicated page for *Cowboy Corner* in every issue, and he also owned a television station in Houston. When I mentioned the idea to him, he suggested we partner on the show. He said he would provide the money if I would put the show together.

We built a set in Greg's television studio and did a variety show called *In the Bunkhouse with Red Steagall*. I had a little four-piece band there in the studio, and I would open every show with a song. Then we would cut to a scene outside where a couple of friends named Bill Cauble and Cliff Teinert were cooking at a chuckwagon. We would see what they were cooking up for a meal that day, and they would explain how they were cooking it. Next, we would come back into the studio, and I would interview someone about the West, just like I was doing on *Cowboy Corner*. It might be an actor, a musician, or an old cowboy, but it always would be somebody who portrayed the West. At some point in the show, I would read a poem, and then we would close each show with a song of inspiration.

We did the first thirteen shows at Greg's station in Houston, and then we moved to the Aztec Theater in Albany, Texas. We did that for four years, and it was going really well. But it eventually got to where I was repeating the songs. I knew the audience was going to get tired of that because I was getting tired of it myself. However, I couldn't find enough original cowboy songs of broadcast quality. A lot of people were writing songs, but they were Hollywood cowboy songs, where they made up scenes and things like that.

Then I started getting emails and letters from people who were commenting on the show. Others would come up to me somewhere and tell me how much they liked the show, but not one of them said, "I liked that poem you read" or "I liked that song you sang." Every one of them would say, "Boy, I love that show. I wish you had kept that old cowboy on a little bit longer. I wanted to hear some more of his stories." And every person who commented, without fail, said, "Thanks for playing the song of inspiration. That means so much to us. It rounds out the story."

I decided if that was what they wanted to hear, then that's what we would do. My friend and cowboy artist Bruce Greene had created a bronze sculpture called *Somewhere West of Wall Street*, and the first time I saw it, I thought, what a great idea for a show. That title covers the whole United States except inside the city limits of New York. I developed a television show called *Red Steagall Is Somewhere West of Wall Street*, opened with an introduction of what the show was going to be about, did a longer interview, and ended with a song of inspiration.

In the beginning, we struggled financially, but a friend named Mike Ingram of Scottsdale, Arizona, jumped in and saved the day. Mike is on the board of directors at the National Cowboy & Western Heritage Museum in Oklahoma City, and he got a group of his friends to chip in and help us. Then, Dennis Carroll, who owned Stetson and Resistol hat companies, Cactus Saddles and Cactus Ropes, and Heel-O-Matic roping dummies, bought a big chunk of commercial time for all of his companies, and we were able to keep going.

If it hadn't been for Mike getting involved in the very beginning, I probably couldn't have stayed on the air because it's expensive to do the show, even though we do it with a skeleton crew. Even today, Mike gets some of our friends to sponsor part of the commercial spot for the National Ranching Heritage Center.

The show now has a life of its own, but we still need support from our friends. We're available in 90 million homes, but we don't ride this trail by ourselves. We always have people we like to say are the kind to ride the river with.

I am very proud of my crew. It's small but mighty. Jim Jennings does the research and writes the story, and there's no one better anywhere to do that. I am so proud to talk to Jim almost every day when we're working. He's a very accomplished writer and a special friend.

I have two cameras, one of which is operated by Jody Duggan, who has spent his life around the rodeo world. Jody knows the Western lifestyle and appreciates it as much as I do. The other camera is operated by Khakie Jo Holland, who grew up in a ranching atmosphere and who also understands the Western lifestyle. As a matter of fact, Khakie breeds bucking bulls for the rodeo business.

Bob Terry is our editor, and he and his wife, Johnie, have been very important in the preservation of the Western lifestyle through their collection of Western toys that at one time were on exhibit at the National Cowboy & Western Heritage Museum. Bob adds a magical touch in making the story come to life on screen.

Bill Zeigler is our road manager and utility man—we couldn't do without him—and my longtime right arm in the office, Debbie Bowman, is our executive assistant. Debbie keeps us all in good shape as far as knowing where we're going, where we're going to stay, and how long we need to be there.

In the very beginning, there were a couple of people who worked on the show but are no longer members of the team. Mike Broyles was our first cameraman and editor, and he was followed by Gary Reynolds, who handled the same positions.

I always close the show by going to the boys on the porch of the bunkhouse for the song of inspiration. Those songs were all recorded at different times, but the four men playing them are some of the most talented musicians in the country. Danny Steagall, Jake Hooker, and Steve Story can play any kind of music, and before Rich O'Brien died, he was a huge part of that group. They are especially good for the song of inspiration. I get lots of compliments on them.

For years, I was preparing myself to do this show and didn't know I was doing it. While the band and I were touring, I sat in the jump seat of that bus and looked out the windshield for miles and miles and miles. I made sure we

A rare photo of my late mother and all her children. (L–R): Barry, David, me, Mother, Sue Anne, Carroll (whom we lost in 2019), and Danny at the National Cowboy Hall of Fame (now the National Cowboy & Western Heritage Museum). (Photo credit Ownbey Photography.)

L–R: The late Dale Robertson, Tom Selleck, the late Maureen O'Hara, Buck Taylor, and me at the National Cowboy Hall of Fame. (Photo credit Ownbey Photography.)

L–R: Famous Western artist, the late Harold "H" Holden, dear friend and Hollywood producer Lincoln Lageson, and me at the National Cowboy Hall of Fame. (Photo credit Ownbey Photography.)

stopped at every historical marker and every museum we came to. If the guys in the band didn't want to get off the bus, they were welcome to stay there and sleep. Several of them would go with me, and we saw the West.

We didn't play enough dates east of the Mississippi to even justify going over there. Everything was west of the Mississippi, primarily in Nebraska, the Dakotas, Wyoming, Montana, Arizona, Colorado, and New Mexico, and a little bit in Oregon, Idaho, Washington, and California. We stopped at any place that was historical.

And I read books about where we were headed. For instance, if we were going up into the Sioux Indian area, I'd find all the books I could about the Sioux Nation. I read about the ranches in the different states and the people who were responsible for the livestock industry in the places we were going to play.

The thing about my background and my education in agriculture is that when I'm interviewing a farmer or a rancher, I know what his problems are, and I know how he faces them. That makes it easy for me to ask him the right questions, get him going in the right direction, and let him tell his story.

George Strait (left) and me at the National Cowboy Hall of Fame for the 60th Annual Western Heritage Awards when he received the Lifetime Achievement Award in 2021.

I hope everybody who is reading this book has seen the show. It's a very simple production, but we try to tell a story and take the viewer along for the ride, and hope they enjoy the trip.

L–R: Me, Gail, and the couple we like to claim as our "kids," Lizzie May and Trent Willmon. Trent is a talented singer, songwriter, and record producer, most notably producing Cody Johnson.

L–R: Me, Gail, and Carol and Dan Roberts at the National Cowboy Hall of Fame.

The best neighbors and friends a fella could have. Shown with me in the front row (L–R), Bill Zeigler and J. D. Morrow. Back row with Gail (L–R), Jill Zeigler and Dianne Morrow.

The youngest artist ever invited to join the prestigious Cowboy Artists of America group, Tyler Crow, honored me by doing this charcoal piece for the annual Cowboy Artists Show, in 2018.

It's worked so far. We're on RFD-TV three times per week, with the primary airing every Monday night, and we're on The Cowboy Channel three times a day, five days a week with reruns. Two thousand twenty-four is our seventeenth year to be on the air, and we have a very large and loyal audience. They love to hear about people, places, and the events in the West, and we try to uncover stories that nobody else is talking about or has ever uncovered. So far, we've done stories all over the West and as far east as Kentucky and Tennessee.

The National Cowboy & Western Heritage Museum presents each year what they call the Western Heritage Awards, which honor individuals who have made significant contributions to Western heritage through creative works in literature, music, television, and film. It's the highest award you can win in our industry, and in the film and television division, *Red Steagall Is Somewhere West of Wall Street* has won the Western Lifestyle Program category five times.

The award presented is a limited-edition bronze sculpture of a cowboy sitting on a horse, and it's called the "Wrangler." It was sculpted by the late Cowboy Artist of America member Harold Holden. For those of us who write and sing cowboy music and cowboy poetry, it's like an Oscar. In addition to the five Wranglers I have won in the film and television division, I have won nine more for my music and poetry.

How I got to know Mike Ingram, who continues to help us with the television show, is an interesting story. I first met Mike years ago in Oklahoma City when he was in the animal health business and was affiliated with the National Finals Rodeo, but we didn't become well acquainted until he moved to Arizona. It all began when Gail and I were in Phoenix at the annual Cowboy Artists of America show, and my good friend, the late, great Cowboy Artist Bill Owen, and his wife Valerie asked us to go with them to a party. The party was hosted by one of Valerie's relatives, and although Gail and I were reluctant to go since we hadn't been invited by the host, I'm glad we did. Valerie's relatives turned out to be Sheila and Mike Ingram, and getting to know them that night was the beginning of the relationship we have today.

Sheila and Mike are very close friends to Gail and me, and they occupy a very large space in our lives. They have a couple of ranches in Montana, where we go twice a year and get to take some of our friends, and we get to meet new friends the Ingrams bring. Every time we go, it turns out to be a unique and wonderful experience.

CHAPTER 15

INSPIRATION

I've already talked about where the inspiration to write some of my songs came from, but many of the songs I have written were inspired by particular events. Bob Wills's music has been important to me all my life because Western swing was what I was playing when I first started recording, and Bob was one of the founders of Western swing. I never had the opportunity to meet Bob because he had already had a stroke and was pretty well incapacitated before I would have been in a position to do so. But I got to know all the men in Bob's band, the Texas Playboys, and I became close to many of them.

I was good friends with Al Stricklin and Leon Rausch, and I just idolized Leon McAuliffe, Smokey Dacus, Joe Frank Ferguson, and Eldon Shamblin. They're all gone now. I'm really proud of a song that involves all those guys. It's called "Bob's Got a Swing Band in Heaven," and how I wrote it is kinda interesting.

In January 1977, the band and I were on our way to the Professional Rodeo Cowboys Association convention in Denver, and Keith Coleman, who played the fiddle in the Texas Playboys, had just died. We went through Cyril, Oklahoma, on our way to Denver, so we could attend Keith's funeral.

They were having the service in the high school auditorium. Behind the curtain, Eldon Shamblin on guitar and Johnny Gimble on fiddle were playing various Bob Wills songs. Then they played "Faded Love," and I'll never forget this as long as I live. The audience started wailing. I don't mean crying, I mean

Me with my good friend Brett Bingham (center) and legendary Texas Playboy, the late Leon Rausch (right).

wailing. That song created so much emotion that they couldn't control themselves. At the end of the song, Johnny walked up to the microphone and said, "Well, I want y'all to know that every fiddle player in America can move up one notch, because God just hired the best one we had."

My first thought was, "I'll bet He's got a whale of a swing band up there." We got back on the bus and headed out, and I wrote "Bob's Got a Swing Band in Heaven" before we reached the end of that little town. It just poured out of me.

It took another week before I really finished it because I added some narration at the end and mentioned all the members of the band who had gone on. I wanted to pay tribute to those who had died.

The band the Original Texas Playboys was organized after Bob Wills's death in 1975. All the members agreed that when one of the Originals died, the band would fulfill their remaining engagements and then disband. Pianist Al Stricklin passed on in October 1986, and the group had its final concert that year in Will Rogers Coliseum in Fort Worth. They let me sing "Bob's Got a Swing Band in Heaven" at the end of it.

About a week later, we did a special tribute to Keith Coleman in Tulsa, and they had me open the show with that song. It meant so much that those guys agreed with me. I'm really proud of it.

Today, the Texas Playboys are still going strong under the direction of my good friend Jason Roberts.

People are always asking me, "Can you write a poem about this or a song about that?" and my answer usually is no, because I don't write on demand. I have to be enthused about it. Something about the subject matter has to touch me inside, emotionally.

I have not finished at least a thousand songs because they just did not have any emotion. If they don't make me proud and make me feel good, I can't use them to make somebody else proud and feel good. I have to see the whole movie. That's the reason I like storyline songs, because I can see the whole movie and I can write it from start to finish. Then I can spend as long as I want polishing it and massaging it. One thing I learned a long time ago—and anybody who writes songs or writes anything will tell you this—never get married to a line. Always leave it open to change and reinterpretation.

Almost everybody who writes, whether it's song, poetry, or literature, knows that you have to write the best line you can possibly write. I've mentioned this before, but a perspective that I've lived with as long as I can remember is something I read when I was a child. It is the quote from John Deere, who, in 1856, said, "I will never put my name on a product that does not have in it the best that is in me." This is a lesson that I try to remember in any artistic endeavor.

I sometimes wake up in the middle of the night and write down lines that are in my mind. If I don't get up and write them down, they're gone by morning. It makes me so dadgum mad, because I know they were the right line. I have a song called "I Ride for the Brand of the Man with the Nail Scarred Hand," and I wrote nearly all of that song at night. Something would inspire me in the middle of the night to write a particular line that I was having trouble with, and I would get up and write it down, and it fit.

I also know that sometimes a greater being or a greater power guides my hand when I'm writing, and that greater power influences my mind to think of the things to write down. I know that because sometimes they come out of nowhere.

Usually, if I write something, especially a poem, it's based on something that I've seen or heard, but not always. I wrote a poem called "McCorkle and the Wire," about a ghost rider. I don't know where it came from, but I wrote it in just a few minutes because it was a vivid picture in my mind.

I can't tell you how I write songs or how I write poems. I hate to sit down and be an instructor, try to teach somebody how to write poetry or music, because everybody's different. Every songwriter will tell you that they have a certain structure in their mind when they start to write. What makes a song palatable to other people and more successful is that there's a perfect marriage between the lyrics and the subject matter, and you have the right melody to portray the lyrics in the proper way. It's a marriage of all the developmental and creative factors.

Just the other day, a lady asked me to write a foreword to a book she's doing. It's about a particular ranch that I'm very familiar with, but I told her that I didn't know that I could do that, because I can't write on demand. Then I got to thinking about all the things I know about that ranch, and the beauty of it and the animals, and the reminiscing, and how you need to pass those impressions on to future generations. I wrote the foreword in about twenty minutes. It's a blessing.

It depends on what I'm working on. If I'm writing a poem, the lines to the poem will just appear. If it's a song, it'll be the lyrics to that song. I'm not as good a musician and composer as I am a lyricist. I love to write the words to a song and then have somebody else do the music that fits. I just don't trust myself to write good melodies all the time.

CHAPTER 16

EXPERIENCES

I have had so many blessed happenings in my life. I have already talked about some of them, but there are lots more. For instance, in 1973, I was booked to play a fair in Orland, California, in the north part of the state. We finished the show, and I sent the boys on back in the van. I needed to go to Los Angeles on some business, and I had to figure out a way to get there.

Orland was a small town at that time, and there were no motels, so they put me up with a family who lived there. The man's name was Pug Baker. I explained my problem to him, and he told me that he and his wife had another house guest I hadn't met yet. That man was going to fly down to Van Nuys, California, in an old Ford Trimotor airplane the next day. "He's a good pilot," Mr. Baker said. "Why don't you just fly down there with him?"

So I did. The Ford Trimotors were made back in the 1920s, and that old plane bucked and jumped around and made a lot of noise, but this guy seemed very confident and knew what he was doing. I sat up front with him, and he talked to me about all the instruments and about flying. I had a good time.

We landed at Van Nuys, and as I unbuckled my seat belt, I turned to him and said, "I sure appreciate you letting me come with you." Then I asked him, "Now, what was your name?"

He said, "I'm Chuck Yeager."

Brigadier General Chuck Yeager was an Air Force officer, flying ace, and record-setting test pilot who in 1947 became the first pilot in history to break

L–R: Ben Crenshaw, Josh Gatlin, Larry Gatlin, Willie Nelson, and me at the Ben-Willie-Darrell Golf Tournament in Austin, mid-1980s.

Longtime college friends Verena (left) and Bruce Thompson (right), the inventor and owner of Sand-X Processes, with me and Gail.

Two of my longtime friends, legendary vocalists Larry Gatlin (left) and the late, great B. J. Thomas (right), at a golf tournament.

the sound barrier. I knew who Chuck Yeager was, but I had no idea I was sitting beside him that morning.

•

Golf has meant a lot to me over the years and still does. I started playing golf as a kid back in Sanford, and I continued to play after I lost the use of my left arm. I could still hit the ball, just maybe not as far as I could have if I had had full use of my arm.

I played a lot of golf when I lived in California and continued to do so after I moved to Parker County, Texas, northwest of Fort Worth. In 2011, Gail and I joined a group of fourteen investors and purchased a community golf club in Aledo, which is also in Parker County. We call it Split Rail Golf Club, and being part owner of a course that's only fifteen minutes from our ranch has been tremendous. It gives me a way to unwind on the few days that I'm home.

I have four friends I love to play with. We don't gamble, we just encourage each other to hit a good shot. Those friends are Kirk Teegarden, Chris Benedict,

Dick McHargue and Bill Badeaux. We enjoy each other's company and the day of golf.

In the late 1970s, throughout the 1980s, and into the early 1990s, I played in celebrity golf tournaments that were hosted by Coach Darrell Royal of the Texas Longhorns. Later, Coach Royal involved Willie Nelson, and then Ben Crenshaw. The first tournament was on Galveston Island, and it was hosted by brothers Johnny and George Mitchell at the Galveston Golf and Country Club to benefit the Boys and Girls Clubs of Galveston. Coach Royal loved songwriters, so he invited lots of them to play in the tournament. We had people like Red Lane, Whitey Shafer, Hank Cochran, and many others, as well as musicians who would come out of Nashville.

When George Mitchell built the Woodlands Golf and Country Club near Houston, we played there. Then we moved it to the Austin Country Club in Austin, Texas.

One time, they put me in a cart with a man from Victoria, Texas, named Claud Jacobs. Claud hosted a tournament in Victoria for the Bluebonnet Youth Ranch at Yoakum, Texas, and he asked if I would be co-celebrity chairman. The other co-celebrity chairman was a woman golfer named Shirley Furlong. We did that for twenty-five years and raised lots of money for that wonderful children's home. After Shirley and I retired, Moe Bandy and Eldon Shamblin were the co-hosts until they discontinued the tournament because the structure of that children's home was changed.

The relationships I developed while playing at Coach Royal's tournaments were life-changing. And all those acts out of Nashville loved those tournaments. They would come all the way to Galveston, the Woodlands, Austin, and Victoria to play in those tournaments. We had some great times. Playing at those country clubs was a long way from where I started playing, at that nine-hole course in Sanford with the sand greens, I assure you.

One time back in the 1970s, I was entered in the Music City Golf Tournament in Nashville, and it was one of those tournaments where you draw partners. I drew Mickey Mantle, a Baseball Hall of Famer who was one of the greatest players who ever lived. Mickey had flown up from Texas to play in that tournament, and he brought along a friend he played golf with all the time. The friend drew Whitey Ford, who was also in the Baseball Hall of Fame. I didn't know any of those three guys, but that was our foursome.

As we were about to start playing, Mickey's friend said, "Okay, Mickey, our regular game, $2 a hole?

I wish I could remember the names of these players, but I do remember that I'm the guy in the red shirt with the red beard (fourth from right) and my dear friend, the late Mickey Mantle, is to the right of me in the picture.

Mickey said, "Yeah."

Now, I didn't have a dime; I was flat broke. But Mickey said, "It's okay, we can beat them. Don't worry about it."

We finish the first nine holes, and we're up six bets. I'm thinking, "Six times two, that's $12, I'm sure I can handle that if we lose." Then this guy says, "Okay, Mantle, our regular bet on the back nine, double?"

Mickey says, "Sure," and then he tells me, "Don't worry about it, we're up six bets, that's just $4 and we're going to whip them anyway."

So, we're playing really well, and we get to the eighteenth green. I've got about a four-foot putt, and Mickey comes over to me and kinda in a low voice, says, "Don't miss that sumbitch; it's worth $3,600 apiece." Then it hit me: we were playing for $200 and $400 a hole, not $2 and $4.

Of course, I missed it, but we still won $600 apiece, which was a big payday to me.

Mickey turned out to be a huge fan and a dear friend, and we played a lot of golf together. He was a member of Preston Trail Golf Club in Dallas, and I would meet him over there. Sometimes, he would get on the bus with us and be gone for up to two weeks at a time while we were doing shows. Mickey and I played tournaments in Hawaii, Mexico, and many other places in the United States. Mickey was so competitive he was unbelievable, and he could knock the ball a mile—he just didn't always know what direction it was going.

•

In 1978, I decided to try something new. I started putting on dances in National Guard armories. In the beginning, I didn't know what it was going to cost, but I knew that Bob Wills did it during the Depression. I figured I could do it, too.

I booked the shows, did my own advertising, paid the band, bought their meals and paid for their lodging, and it ended up costing me $3,800 a dance. Each dance brought in about $2,300, so that obviously didn't add up.

In 1979, the *For All My Cowboy Friends* album had been out a couple of years, and a guy who was running a record company in Australia told me that it was the biggest thing going down there; he said we needed to come down. So I hired a guy to go and scout it all out. I bought him two pairs of Leddy's boots, three suits, and a new Resistol hat to make the trip. He came back and told me, "I got twenty-nine out of the first thirty days booked, and then they'll see what else they can do."

I decided that would work, so I booked a trip to Australia for me and the band. When we landed, our agent down there met us in the airport. I said, "It's pretty good, starting out twenty-nine out of thirty days."

He looked at me and said, "Red, I've only got one day out of thirty."

I'm sure he could tell I was shocked, and then he said, "But I do have a two-week deal at the Cross Keys Hotel in Essendon. You'll play five nights a week in the ballroom, and they'll give you free lodging and meals."

I couldn't do anything else; I was stuck down there. Then I met a guy named John Singleton, who had a television show, and he hired us to play on his show. He also wanted me to play a rodeo at Kooralbyn, up close to Brisbane. He flew us up there in his plane, so we got to see the Outback from the air, which was a unique view of the countryside.

When we got there, we still had a few days before the rodeo, so I decided I was going to rent a car and drive up to Adelaide. I knew of a guy who ranched near Mount Widderin who had bought seventeen daughters of the great Quarter Horse Hollywood Gold when B. F. Phillips Jr. had his first dispersal sale, and he had bought a son of Doc Bar called Poco Poco Doc. Hollywood Gold was one of the foundation sires of the Four Sixes Ranch, and Doc Bar is considered to be one of the greatest sires of cutting horses of all time. I wanted to see those horses.

The man had a beautiful place, and those horses looked like they had been stamped from a cookie cutter. They were the most beautiful things ever, and I was glad I got to see them. But what's interesting is that there was no place to stay up there, so we spent the night in his front yard on blankets.

On the way back, we stopped at a phone booth and I called this agent. I told him where we were and he said, "Oh, I'm so glad you called. I had no way to get in touch with you. You have to get back here. Pan American Airways called me this morning. They made a mistake on your tickets. If you don't leave in the morning, it's going to cost you $1,900 each."

I had already lost about $30,000, and I sure wasn't going to take a chance on losing another $1,900 a man, so we had to end our Australia trip. But I'm glad we went. That was one of the great trips of my life, where I learned things that I would never have learned any other way.

•

I have been in several movies, but most people have never seen the majority of them. I did a song in *Vanishing Point* with Barry Newman, but I had parts in *Shadows on the Wall* with Wilford Brimley and Rex Linn, in *Abilene* with Ernie Borgnine, and in *Dark Before Dawn* with Eddie Gaylord. That last one also had rodeo announcer Clem McSpadden and my good friend Buck Taylor in it. I've been fortunate that I've had some other opportunities as well.

In 1974, a movie director and screenwriter by the name of Joe Camp released a movie about a stray dog named Benji. The film had been turned down by every studio in Hollywood, and Joe had to form his own film company to distribute the picture worldwide. However, the movie ended up grossing $45 million on a budget of $500,000, and its theme song received an Oscar nomination for Best Original Song.

Joe went on to produce four more of the Benji movies, and I starred in one of them. I was the hunter who captured Benji in *Benji the Hunted*, which was released in 1987.

Benji the Hunted movie poster, circa 1987. I was one of only two humans in the film.

It all started in 1985 when some mutual friends introduced me to Joe, and I learned what he did. I had been wanting to produce a movie on Freckles Brown and his ride on Tornado, and I saw this as an opportunity. Joe wasn't interested in the Freckles Brown idea, but he suggested I write the music for *Benji the*

Hunted, which was going to be his next Benji movie. I told him I would, and I wrote a couple of songs.

As it turned out, the songs I wrote didn't touch him much, but a couple of days later, he called and said there was a small part in the movie that he thought I would fit. He wanted to know if I would be interested. He said, "You would be one of only two humans in the movie, and you wouldn't be on camera but about ten or twelve times. All I have to pay you is $2,500, and we would be filming in Oregon. You would have to pay your own transportation up there."

Even though it wouldn't be much money, I told him I would do it. I thought it was important to my career. We spent six weeks along the Oregon coast filming that movie, but it just so happened that I had four rodeos already booked during those six weeks. I had to take the weekends off and fly out of Eugene, Oregon, to go play those rodeos. My expenses in doing that were more than double what Joe paid me, but I learned a lot about the movie business, just watching Joe, going to all the production meetings that I could get to, and listening to what they were talking about.

That was useful, but it was good in other ways, too. The movie grossed $22 million, and because I was one of the only humans in the movie, the residuals I received made a significant difference in our lives. I owe a big debt of gratitude to the late Joe Camp for this incredible opportunity.

In 1988, I was at a golf tournament in Joplin, Missouri, and after the tournament, I was sitting at a table with Jimmy Dean. I told Jimmy that I was trying to put together a deal to do a movie on Freckles Brown, and Jimmy said, "Why don't we do a movie on Big Bad John? I've already got a guy working on a script."

"Big Bad John" was a song written and recorded by Jimmy Dean. It was released in September 1961, and by the beginning of November it had gone to No. 1 on the Billboard Hot 100. It won Jimmy the 1962 Grammy Award for Best Country & Western Recording and was nominated for the Grammy Award for Song of the Year.

Sitting there at that table, thinking about what I had learned from Joe Camp and from walking around the movie sets at Samuel Goldwyn Studios with Burt Lancaster, I said, "Well, I think I know how to put that together."

He said, "You do?"

"I think so."

He said, "Well then, let's do it."

Jimmy and I began by putting all the pieces where they belonged. We took that script and honed it down, rewrote it and got it like we wanted it, and then I went to Hollywood and hired Burt Kennedy as director. Burt was a successful writer and director who had worked on a number of Westerns.

Next, we put a production crew together and went on location to Caddo Lake, on the Texas-Louisiana border, south of Texarkana. It was a beautiful place to film the first part of that show. We went from there to Trinidad, Colorado, and finished the show in one of those old coal mines up there.

I was the producer, and I learned a lot about production and about handling people in production teams. They all have their own personalities, and they all have their own ideas about what their job is.

Among the actors in the movie were Jimmy Dean, Ned Beatty, Jack Elam, Bo Hopkins, Buck Taylor, Annie Lockhart, and Doug English, who played the part of Big Bad John. I also had a part in the movie, and I was proud of it. We knew it was not going to be a box office sensation, but we thought we could get the money back. As it happened, we tried to come out at a time when all the major producers were like Pac-Man, eating up all the independent producers; it wasn't a place for us.

That was the climate that developed while we were on location. By the time I got back to Hollywood and started trying to find a way to market the film, nobody would talk to me.

We released *Big Bad John*, the movie, in 1990, and we didn't make a dime on it, but we had a good time doing it. However, I haven't done another one since.

•

In 2000, I got a call from Woody Gilliland, one of my fraternity brothers at West Texas State. Woody was retired from the Marines and was serving as executive director of the West Texas Rehabilitation Center in Abilene, Texas.

I was familiar with the West Texas Rehab Center, and I knew that my good friend Rex Allen had been the honorary chairman of the center for years. However, Rex had died, and Woody was calling to see if I would accept the position. I jumped on it.

The West Texas Rehabilitation Center is an outstanding organization, and I wanted to be a part of it. They provide outpatient physical therapy, occupational therapy, speech therapy, audiology, orthotics, prosthetics, and hospice care. They serve thousands of children and adults, and they don't turn anyone down. They

Me and Neal McCoy ready to go onstage in Abilene, Texas at the West Texas Rehab Telethon.

Me and The Boys in The Bunkhouse onstage at the West Texas Rehab Telethon, Abilene, Texas, in 2014.

raise money through donations and auctions so those without insurance or the financial means to pay for the care can still receive it.

In addition to the Abilene location, there are facilities in two other West Texas towns, San Angelo and Ozona, but in January each year the operations all come together for a telethon and auction. In the beginning, it was strictly a livestock auction, where local ranchers donated livestock to be sold. But the auction has become a lot more than that. Today, donation items range from handmade quilts and homemade cookies to guided hunting and fishing trips to automobile repair, guns, art, and even rodeo tickets. The range is endless, and you can't imagine how much money a plate of homemade cookies brings.

For close to twenty-five years, I have been the honorary chairman of Roundup for Rehab. I appear on the telethon each year, and Gail and I are extremely proud to be a part of the organization. I have made lots of friends who mean the world to me, and in addition to working with the telethon and the other big functions, I really enjoy going out to the smaller communities where we have sales that benefit the Rehab Center. The general manager and president of all the West Texas Rehab Centers is Steve Martin. He and his wife Kelly have become very close friends as well as being a real pleasure to work with.

CHAPTER 17

AWARDS AND RECOGNITION

I've had a great life. I settled in North Texas, not very far from where my ancestors lived when they first came to Texas in 1870. I love North Texas; I love the people who live here. I do a good job entertaining myself playing golf and riding horses, and I'm still working. I have a weekly radio show and a weekly television show, and I still make a number of personal appearances every year.

Gail and I wound up buying a little ranch out west of Fort Worth, where we could keep our horses. For several years, we were active in the cutting horse business. Then, at one point, we got into the Longhorn business, but we had only 100 acres and about twenty-five cows. That didn't work very long: the grass was gone pretty quickly.

So we got rid of the cattle, but we still have our horses. I've traveled all over the world, met people in all walks of life, been to places that I never dreamed I'd go to, even when I was watching that Texas Silver Zephyr go across the plains. That train couldn't have taken me to the Middle East or the Pacific Rim or South America or Europe. I've been a very fortunate boy. I'm grateful for every single minute of it, but I know life's not over. There are a lot of other things I haven't done that I'm going to get a chance to experience.

Me and Robert Duvall at a Texas Rangers Law Enforcement Convention when he was awarded an honorary badge.

I got involved in the agricultural community through working on the various big ranches I've been associated with. I say working, but I wasn't really working; I was staying out of the way. I sure had a good time. I had the opportunity to stay out with the chuckwagon, sleeping on the ground in my tepee and learning the vernacular of the cowboys while watching their actions. Because of those opportunities, I know that when I write about the cowboys—and I write about them a lot—what I'm writing is authentic.

And that's important. I honestly believe that fifty years from now, the only way people will have a real idea of how we lived is from the things we write and record today. We must do it authentically, because what we say becomes gospel.

As I mentioned earlier, I have won fourteen Western Heritage Awards from the National Cowboy & Western Heritage Museum in Oklahoma City for my music, poetry, and television show. But one day, I got a call from the Cowboy Hall that said, "You have been selected for induction into the Hall of Great Westerners at the Cowboy Hall of Fame."

You could have blown me away. I mean, I was just overwhelmed, and it's still one of the great tributes of my life. Then, in late 2022, the Cowboy Hall called and told me that in the spring of 2023, I would receive the Lifetime Achievement Award. Again, I was caught totally by surprise. Only four other people had ever been presented with that award: Michael Martin Murphey, world-renowned recording artist; the late Linda Davis, the matriarch of the CS Ranch in New Mexico and a leader in the ranching industry for more than sixty years; Robert Duvall, a legendary actor and a star in several Western movies including, of course, *Lonesome Dove*; and George Strait, the undisputed king of country music. I never could have imagined that I would be included with those four legends, and I owe a lot to Dan Roberts and Gary Pratt, who nominated me for the award. (In 2024, my dear friend Reba McEntire was presented with the Lifetime Achievement Award, and I was so proud to have been asked to present it to her.)

Now, when you add those last two honors, that makes sixteen Wranglers I have received. I have them sitting all over my living room.

Starting about 1991, Fort Worth media partners sponsored the Charles Goodnight Gala as a fundraising effort for local charities. Many notable Westerners who are committed to preserving Western heritage and livestock traditions have been honored with the award bearing Goodnight's name. I won that award in 2006, and it's one of my greatest thrills. I was also the 2023 Amarillo Tri-State Fair and Rodeo Western Heritage Award winner. That award honors those who have made significant contributions to the agriculture community in the Texas Panhandle, where I grew up.

I have been blessed to have been inducted into several halls of fame, including the Texas Cowboy Hall of Fame, the Texas Rodeo Cowboy Hall of Fame,

L–R: The late Dr. Glenn Blodgett, me, and Johnny Trotter at the unveiling of the Anne Marion bronze and plaques, sculpted by artist Bruce Greene, at the National Ranching Heritage Center in Lubbock, Texas.

the Old Time Music Hall of Fame, the Colorado Music Hall of Fame, and the Texas Country Music Hall of Fame. I'm proud of them all, but that last one is special because I'm there with my buddies Tex Ritter and Jim Reeves, and all the other people from Texas who have contributed to America's music.

Every single one of those awards is more important than the last one, but to be recognized by your peers in whatever endeavor you're in gives you a lift up and makes you know that what you're doing is good, and you can go forward.

L–R: I'm laughing it up with my pals Larry Work, Joel Nelson, and Tio Kleberg at the National Ranching Heritage Center.

In 2018, I won the National Golden Spur Award at the National Ranching Heritage Center in Lubbock, Texas. That was a tremendous honor because that award has been presented annually for more than fifty years to some of the most prestigious ranchers across this country, and I'm the only recipient who wasn't a rancher.

The National Ranching Heritage Center (NRHC) is very important to me. That facility, which is located on the campus of Texas Tech University, is a museum and historical park that is dedicated to the preservation of the history of ranching. It features fifty-five historic structures there that were relocated, restored, and furnished for period correctness, and they show the evolution of ranch life from the late 1700s through the mid-1900s.

There are also forty-two life-size bronze outdoor art pieces and a museum that showcases permanent as well as temporary exhibits of art, photography, and artifacts that capture historical and contemporary Western life.

The NRHC is where I want to leave my collection of Western artifacts, along with all the manuscripts that are associated with the songs and poems I have written and the radio and television shows I have produced. As a result, the Red Steagall Institute for Traditional Western Arts has been established.

But it's not going to be just my things. It will be a repository for other artists and writers as well, and it will be a place to learn. Each discipline in the Institute will have its own society, and the best artisans in the country at the time will be inducted into their respective societies. There will be a society for those recognized as masters in the written word, to include poetry and music, and there will be societies recognizing masters in wall-hung art, to include all the media associated with wall-hung art. There will also be societies for those involved in sculpture, bit-and-spur making, and leather working.

We will recognize in the societies the people who are alive today; we won't dwell on people who have gone on before. We'll learn from them, but we want this to be a living institute for the people who are performing those art forms today.

There will be an opportunity for aspiring young artists from all over the United States to come to the campus at certain times of the year and study with one of the masters. Music and poetry will be presented to the public at various times throughout the year, and there will be a research library that will be available to both scholars and students to study the American West.

I'm probably more fond of the research library than anything else, because one day it will be the most important place in the country to learn about the West. It will give us a chance to show future generations who we are and how we've protected the integrity of the Western lifestyle, to include the heritage, the traditions, and especially the set of values by which we try to live.

The late master spur maker Billy Klapper's entire shop will be recreated in the Institute, as will the saddle shops of Carl Darr and Tooter Cannon, both of whom were well known for building tack for ranch cowboys. There will be spur makers and saddle makers working in those shops, and those craftsmen will be available to talk to visitors about the work they are doing.

The purpose of the National Ranching Heritage Center is to provide visitors with an authentic feel of ranching. I want the Red Steagall Institute to be an integral part of that.

CHAPTER 18

HORSES I'VE RODE AND PEOPLE I'VE KNOWED

Horses have always been important to me, even as far as back as when, as a 5-year-old, I watched those Sanford Ranch cowboys trot through my hometown. I wasn't able to own a horse until after I moved to California and had some success as a songwriter, but when I moved from there to Tennessee, I took my horses with me.

Gail and I bought our little ranch west of Fort Worth in the fall of 1977, and I immediately began thinking of horses. I had a lot of friends who were in the cutting horse business, people like Bud Swayze, Bobby Shelton, Jim Reno, Lloyd Brinkman, Dick Gaines, and many more, so I started thinking about raising cutting horses.

At that time, I still had the band on a salary. I had to pay them whether we worked or not. I came up with a plan as to how I could build a small broodmare band and breed to some of the best stallions in the cutting horse industry. Going to the top breeders, I offered to play a dance at a party or a horse sale in return for a nice mare that would improve my broodmare band or for a breeding to one of their top stallions. As a result, I was able to put together a nice band of seven mares, which I bred every year to the most important stallions in the cutting horse industry, including Docs Lynx, Doc Tari, Doc Quixote, and Docs Hickory. Then I sold those foals, usually as yearlings.

There would be times during the year when, in addition to the seven mares, I would have seven weanlings and maybe seven yearlings. It got to be quite a job to handle all of that, especially when I was on the road 250 days a year. But I love the horse business, and I love to watch those babies grow. You can tell what kind of adults they're going to make because of their muscle conformation, the way they move, their attitude, whether they have a good calm eye or whether they're constantly looking for something to be boogered about.

There was one horse in particular that I was really proud of, and I'll never forget him. My friend Lloyd Brinkman, who had a ranch at Kerrville, Texas, had a herd of Brangus cattle, which he operated as Brinks Brangus. He was also in the Quarter Horse business in a big way. He had an exceptional band of broodmares, as fine as anybody had ever put together anywhere in the industry, and he had some great stallions.

One day he called and wanted me to play for a party he was having in conjunction with his horse sale. He said, "I'll give you your pick of the yearling colts."

Don Jones, who was the former executive secretary of the American Quarter Horse Association, was running the horse outfit for him, and I felt like he knew what a good horse was supposed to look like. Brink told Don, "Take Red out to the barn. I promised him his pick of the yearlings."

There were about 150 of them, but I saw only one horse. I mean the instant I saw him, I never looked at anything else. He was the most beautiful animal I had ever seen in my life. I pointed at a red dun colt kinda standing by himself and told Don, "I want that one right there."

"Well, that's a good one," he said. "He's by Mr Spanish Lee by Leo out of a mare named Tiana Bar by Steel Bars. He'll make a good horse."

We got back to the house and Brink asked, "Well, did you find Red a horse?"

Don said, "Yes, he got a good one."

Maybe it was because of the tone of Don's voice, but with a puzzled look on his face, Brink asked, "Which one is it?"

Bandito Gold, 1979 AQHA National High Point Western Pleasure Horse—my pride and joy.

Don said, "It's that son of Mr Spanish Lee."

"Oh, I intended for you to hide him," Brink said, and then he turned to me. "Okay, you've got a good horse, but you've got to leave him here for a year. At

L–R: Cowboy Artist Fred Fellows, the late author Don Hedgpeth, me, and the late cowboy artists Bill Owen and Joe Beeler on the fence at the 6666 branding.

next year's sale, I'll have him in a pen with your name on it. That will give me some credibility that you like my horses."

I didn't know why that would be important to him, but I was thrilled. I don't remember what the horse's registered name was, but I had AQHA change it to Bandito Gold, which was the name of a song I had written for the rodeo album. It just seemed to fit him.

The next year, I had Charles Crawley, who was a trainer from Georgia, come look at the colt, and Charles took him home to start him in training. In 1979, as a 3-year-old, Bandito Gold was the AQHA high-point junior Western pleasure horse for the year. Early the next year, Charles qualified him for the AQHA World Championship Show in five events.

I sold him later that year. I didn't need a stallion, didn't want to be in the stallion business, and a man from North Carolina offered me more money for him than I thought there was in the whole world. I've regretted it ever since.

One time, I was performing at the rodeo during the Dixie National at Jackson, Mississippi, and Charles had Bandito Gold there for the horse show. I

Neighbor and super friend Bill Zeigler (left) and me with legendary lawman, McClennan County Sheriff Parnell McNamara (right) at the 6666 Ranch in Guthrie, Texas.

rode him into the rodeo arena, got off and did my show, got back on him, and rode out of the arena.

I did very well with my horses until the bottom dropped out of the industry in 1983. Horses that had been worth a lot of money suddenly were not worth nearly as much. I sold everything except for one mare that I really liked, and I've had some nice foals out of her in the ensuing years.

I've still got one broodmare that I breed every other year, and I've also got a couple of geldings that I've roped on and that I ride when I'm invited to brandings at some of the big ranches around the state. It was about the time that I first got in the horse business that I started going to the Four Sixes for spring works. That's where I learned how to write about the people that I love the most, those people in the livestock industry and the agricultural community. I've always kept horses that I could use to ride in that old rough country and work cattle, drag calves to the fire and enjoy riding.

That's about the extent of my horse business, but I still love it. It's a good thing I don't have a lot of money, because if I did, I would spend every dime of it on horses and a place to keep them.

Of course, when I was on the road so much, we had to have help with the horses and with the ranch in general, and we've been blessed through the years with great help. Bobby Johnston was our manager for more than twenty years and raised his family on our ranch. The Mark Spillman family was here for several years. Patrick Starrett was a big help for three years, as was Anthony Sheridan. Currently, Brady Graham manages our outfit, and we feel lucky to have him on board.

•

Before I end this book, I have got to give thanks to certain people who changed the direction of my life. Some of those people are gone now, but some are still with us, and most of them have no idea of the influence they had on me. As a matter of fact, even I didn't know how I was being influenced by most of these people until later in my life when I had the opportunity to look back. Many of them have already been mentioned in one form or another earlier in the book, but I'm not sure I emphasized their influence enough.

The first one, and probably the most important, was my mother. She raised six of us pretty well by herself, and there's not a failure among us. She recognized that when I had polio, I was going to have special challenges I would face for the rest of my life. She instilled in me the idea that there was nothing I couldn't do if I wanted it bad enough, despite my handicap. She gave me the desire to do whatever I wanted to do, and she taught me how to face head on the obstacles I was going to meet. I idolized her then, and I still do.

The next person who influenced me was my uncle Floyd Schleusener. Uncle Floyd was a farmer in Iowa, and a good one. I spent five summers on that farm with him and Aunt Johnie, and I've said a million times how I learned more in those five summers than I have all the rest of my life. I don't mean only how to farm, although I definitely learned a lot about farming. Uncle Floyd was a farmer who wanted to do the best job he possibly could. Raising a crop was not good enough for him; it had to be the best crop he could get out of that ground. As a result, Uncle Floyd taught me not to be satisfied with "good enough." He also showed me how to put my life in order, and he made me realize that my destiny depended on me and no one else.

The minister in the church we attended while I was growing up, Newton Starnes, had a tremendous influence on me. He made me want to be in the front pew of the Wesley United Methodist Church in Borger every Sunday. With Reverend Starnes's urging, I even preached in some of the area churches when the regular pastor was on vacation, and I enjoyed it a lot. At the time, I considered becoming a preacher, but then I realized that what I enjoyed about it was that the people in the church were listening to me. In other words, I was on stage, and I liked that. But I didn't think that was what the Lord had in mind. I moved on to another career, and I suspect Reverend Starnes approved. I do, however, remember him very fondly for the lessons he instilled in me.

The next person who really changed my life was Jimmy Bowen, and just maybe, other than my mother, Jimmy is more responsible for where I am today than any other single person. He is the one who set me on the path to having the career I have had for the past sixty or so years.

I knew Jimmy in college when several of us were trying to be musicians. When we graduated, I had a degree in animal science and agronomy, and I went to work in the agricultural chemistry field. Jimmy and my childhood friend Donnie Lanier met Buddy Knox at West Texas State College and together they formed the group Buddy Knox and the Rhythm Orchids and had a stellar career in the world of rockabilly music. Jimmy then went to Hollywood and became the most important producer in the recording industry. Donnie followed Jimmy to Hollywood; a couple of years later they gave me the opportunity to join them. Jimmy took me in and began teaching me about the music business. In the beginning, I was selling industrial chemicals just to make a living, but he allowed me to hang out with him and others who were working in the recording industry. Then, when my friend Eddie Reeves helped me get a job at United Artists Music, because of my association with Jimmy I was able to get through doors that the average person could never get enter. Later on, Jimmy and I were in the music business together. He dramatically

L–R: Me, Gail, the late Parker County rancher Philip French, wife CK French, Nan Kingsley, and longtime friend and host of American Country Countdown and CT40, the late Bob Kingsley.

changed the direction of my life; he gave me an idea of what I wanted to do and how to do it.

Another big influence on my life started while I was in California. There I met Bob Kingsley and his wife, Nan. Bob and I became friends when I first moved to Hollywood, and we went everywhere together. He invited me to join the Academy of Country and Western Music, and that's where I met people like Gene Autry, Roy Rogers, Jimmy Wakely, Eddie Dean, Tex Williams, Tex Ritter, and so many more. The name of the organization was changed to the Academy of Country Music, and I became chairman of it. Being able to associate with all those stars greatly expanded my horizons. But they weren't stars to me, they were my friends. We ate breakfast together and we went hunting together, and I learned so much about the music business from all of them.

Later, after I moved to Texas, Bob and Nan helped me start *Cowboy Corner*. Bob is gone now, but Nan is still a partner on the show with Gail and me.

The next event that really made a difference in the direction my life took was when I met Walt Garrison and Ernie Taylor in Amarillo, Texas, at the

Sharing the excitement of Reba McEntire's first gold album.

Tepee Western Store. As I mentioned in chapter 8, this was my intro into the world of professional rodeo. Walt had been a tremendous running back for the Dallas Cowboys, and he was the chief spokesman for U.S. Tobacco with their Copenhagen and Skoal products. U.S. Tobacco was a major sponsor of professional rodeo. With Walt that day was Ernie Taylor, who was the current world champion calf roper. They were headed for Oklahoma City and the National

My hero, the late Ben Johnson (left), and me.

My longtime pal, Tanya Tucker. Her dad, Beau, hired me to entertain at her 18th birthday party in Fort Worth.

Finals Rodeo, and they asked me to go with them. I did, and that trip truly changed my life. It was during that trip that I met Freckles Brown and wrote the song about him, which led me to become a part of the rodeo world. For the next twenty years, I played rodeos all across this country.

It was also that year at the National Finals Rodeo that I met Reba McEntire. Reba gives me credit for launching her career, and I guess maybe I did, but my friendship and association with her have expanded my horizons way beyond what I might have done for her. Reba has opened a ton of doors for me that she doesn't even know about.

Walt Garrison, at that time, was married to B. F. Phillips Jr.'s daughter Pam, and through Walt I got to know B. F. At dinner one night with B. F. and his wife Anne, who was the heir to the famous Four Sixes Ranches, I was invited to the Sixes for spring works. I went, and I continued to go for the next twenty-eight years. Being around the cowboys opened up a whole new world that I knew existed but didn't have enough education to write about. Being able to spend those years on that ranch changed all that.

I was able to do the same thing on the JA Ranch in the Texas Panhandle. Ranch owner Ninia Ritchie allowed me to go there, take guys with me, and experience a real working relationship with the cowboys, the animals, and the land. Because of my experiences on those two ranches, I have to thank B. F., Anne, Sixes manager J. J. Gibson and his son Mike, current owner Taylor Sheridan, and manager Joe Leathers. And on the JA, I have to thank Ninia, her son Andrew Bivins, ranch manager Jay O'Brien, and the various cowboys we worked with.

There are three more friends, whose names everyone will recognize, who are gone now, but they meant so much to me. I treasured Ben Johnson's friendship more than I can express, and Wilford Brimley was like a brother. Richard Farnsworth was as close as friends can be. I talked to those three guys nearly every week until, one by one, they were gone. The way they influenced my life will live as long as I do.

I mentioned before that it was at the Charles Goodnight Gala in Fort Worth that I met Vickie and Mike Stevens, which led to a big direction change in my life. Mike and Vickie own a company called Farm and Ranch Health Care, which is associated with Heartland Alliance of America. I became executive director of Heartland Alliance, and then president for about twenty years. That really expanded my horizons because I met people in the insurance business that I would never have met otherwise. Many of them became friends I still treasure and will for the rest of my life.

My music made it to outer space in 2002 thanks to shuttle *Endeavor* pilot Paul Lockhart.

Onstage with the late great Charley Pride, my longtime special friend.

The late Charlie Daniels (left), Gail, and me at the National Finals Rodeo.

It was in 1970 that Dave Burgess and I went to the Bob Marshall Wilderness to hunt grizzly bear and elk. I met the famous artist Fred Fellows on that trip, and although I can't explain why, we became like brothers. Fred invited me to attend some functions of the Cowboy Artists of America, including their trail rides. In 1983, the CA made me an honorary member, and becoming a part of that group is one of my biggest satisfactions. All those artists became like family, just like the rodeo people had become my family.

Another of the CA members to whom I became very close is Bruce Greene. Bruce and I have traveled lots of miles together and we, too, have become like brothers.

Still another of the CA artists I came to adore was Bill Owen, who died in 2013. Bill was one of the greatest Western artists the world has ever known, and it was through Bill and his wife Valerie that I met Mike Ingram. Mike and I are very close, and he has done so many things for me, including being responsible for our television show staying on the air. When we needed a major sponsor, he put one together with the board of directors of the National Cowboy & Western Heritage Museum in Oklahoma City.

It's through Mike that I became friends with Kristi Noem, the governor of South Dakota. I think she is one of the finest people I have ever known, and I absolutely admire and adore her.

Cody Johnson and me.

The National Cowboy & Western Heritage Museum is where I met Gary and Deb Kinslow. Gary has been on the board of directors of that museum for years, and he and Deb have added a tremendously positive dimension to our lives. Gary and Deb are entrepreneurs, restauranteurs, and very important people in the world of fast food, and Gary has also been instrumental in keeping our television show on the air.

Me and Gail with our furry family: Dolly, the Papillion; Bonnie Sue, the Mini Aussie; and Sofiejane, the Miniature Schnauzer. (Photo credit Smiley Studios.)

As I look back on my life and the people I associate with today, there are some for whom I can't measure their value to my life and the appreciation and love I have for them. One of those people is Greg Brown. He is my partner in the television show, and he has expanded my horizons in a lot of different areas just because of the people he's associated with.

Another one of my very special friends is Johnny Trotter, who lives in Hereford, Texas. Johnny is a giant feedlot operator and is very influential in the banking industry in the state. I have so much admiration for him as a businessman and as a person, and I just love him and his wife Jana.

Jim Martin, who is the major sponsor of the Cowboy Gathering and a sponsor of the television show, is very important to me. Jim is a realtor by trade, but he is a good all-around guy and a very special friend.

Many of the people I've mentioned are in what I refer to as my brain trust. Everyone needs someone who adds something to their life that's positive, spiritual, and progressive, and I have that. This is a group of guys from different walks of life that I depend on if I need some advice or support. Those are Mike Ingram, because of his ability to see the bigger picture and make something bigger out of something good; Gary Kinslow, whom I admire for his business acumen and his people skills; Johnny Trotter, whom I lean on sometimes for business decisions; Bruce Greene, who is very creative and is always available when I require some creativity; Jim Jennings, who writes the scripts for our television show and whom I always depend on when I need something written; and Greg Brown, my partner in the television show to whom I talk almost every day. I have a lot of wonderful friends that I cherish, but these men are the ones I depend upon to help me make decisions. I'm very fortunate to have this group of guys. I wish everyone was that fortunate.

•

Every good story has an ending, but we've not reached the end of this one yet. Gail and I are both healthy, and we're still going full bore.

We have been partners now for forty-seven years. We make our decisions together. But Gail's not only my partner and my soulmate, she's my best friend. I have had several surgeries through the years, and she's never left my side through any of them. She's been with me in the hospital through it all except for when I had Covid. Of course, she couldn't even come near the hospital then.

As we go forward, we're continually thinking about what we're going to do with the rest of our lives. We're very happy where we are—we love our little ranch, our home, and our friends, and there's not much we're going to change. I certainly don't plan on retiring any time soon. I'm going to keep the radio and television shows on the air as long as I can, and I plan to continue making some appearances.

I've been through a lot in my life, some of which was very good. Then there were times that were not so good. But I don't believe in failure. I didn't let polio conquer me, nor did I give up when I was faced with some of the other things I've been through physically and professionally. I think there's always a way around any kind of obstacle. If you run up against a wall that seems to stop you, you can dig under it, crawl over it, go around the end, or get you a Ford pickup with a good brush guard on the front and knock it down. Quitting is not an option. There ain't no place to go to quit.

All our radio and television shows close with a song of inspiration, and there's a reason for that. My faith in the Lord goes back to the days when as a young child I would fight for a place on the front pew of the Methodist Church. I was always interested in what the preacher had to say, and I loved to learn about the Bible.

I'm going to close this book with a song of inspiration, and it's a special one. I've stated in the book how important it is to ride for the brand, to be loyal to the one for whom you work. The brand we should all pay attention to and ride hard for is in the shape of a cross, and that's where this song came from.

All my life, I have known the Lord was in control. This became even more evident to me when I was working on this song. I would wake up in the middle of the night with a line that I had been searching for, and I would get up and write it down. Because of that, I know I didn't write this one by myself. It's called "I Ride for the Brand of the Man with the Nail Scarred Hands."

"I Ride for the Brand of the Man with the Nail Scarred Hands"

I saddle up each morning
With a grateful heart and mind.
I'm happy and my life is so complete.
As I ride through God's Cathedral
Where His majesty abounds,
I thank Him for his Son who died for me.

When I trail the Oreano
Into places I've not been,
I sometimes feel I'm lost and all alone.
But I let my pony have his head
And put my trust in him,
And like my Lord, he leads me safely home.

And though my day be troubled,
I will still rise up with joy.
I know that I am blessed inside His arms.
He told me if I'd follow Him
And ride the narrow trail,
That He will guide me safely through life's storms.

I have pledged my life to Jesus,
Feel his power in my soul.
I no longer have to fear what I can't see.
I feel as though I've sprouted wings,
I ride the narrow trail,
And strive to be the man He wants of me.

And when it comes my time to go,
And Jesus calls my name
To join the chorus in His angel band,
He'll greet me at the Pearly Gates
And welcome me inside,
'Cause I ride for the brand
Of the Man with the Nail Scarred Hands.

'Cause I ride for the brand
Of the Man with the Nail Scarred Hands.
I once rode with the devil
Through his Hell of burning sand.
Then I found the love of Jesus,
I was saved and born again.
Now I ride for the brand
Of the Man with the Nail Scarred Hands.

Thank you, Lord, for the inspiration.

As my old daddy would say, "We got this one saucered and blowed." Thanks for riding along with me, and thanks for letting me be a part of your world for a little while.

Adios, mis amigos.

APPENDIX

Red's Rangers

Red Steagall – Parker County, Texas
Seth Hopkins – Cartersville, Georgia
Alan Friedman – Dallas, Texas
Roy Gene Evans – Dallas, Texas
Bill Benton – Sherman, Texas
Larry Work – Idalou, Texas
Martin Harrison – Parker County, Texas
Rowland Robinson – Dallas, Texas
Rob Farrell – Dallas, Texas
Jay Evans – Dripping Springs, Texas
Bing Graffunder – Dallas, Texas
Jim Bret Campbell – Lubbock, Texas
Luther King – Fort Worth, Texas
Tom Perini – Buffalo Gap, Texas
Mike Rose – Houston, Texas
Gifford Touchstone – Dallas, Texas
Tony Spears – Gonzales, Texas
Larry Williams – Boise, Idaho
Larry Hobbs – Waco, Texas
Mike Richards – Dallas, Texas
Larry Toon – Dallas, Texas
Bruce Greene – Clifton, Texas

John Kimberlin – Dallas, Texas
Randy Upshaw – Palo Pinto County, Texas
Dr. Ron Goode – Dallas, Texas
Trent Willmon – Nashville, Tennessee
Dan Roberts – Parker County, Texas
Dr. Jim Heird – Parker County, Texas
Gary Kinslow – Prague, Oklahoma
Bill Heard – Dallas, Texas
Tio Kleberg – Kingsville, Texas
Mike Ingram – Scottsdale, Arizona
Greg Brown – Parker County, Texas
Gerald Nobles – Brady, Texas
Sam Hocker – Dallas, Texas
Marc Myers – Dallas, Texas
Cliff Teinert – Albany, Texas
Mike Stevens – Fort Worth, Texas
James Herring – Dallas, Texas
Randy Bloomer – Buda, Texas
Keith Mundee – Bowie, Texas

Honors and Awards

1991

Named "The Official Cowboy Poet of Texas" by Texas State Legislature

1999

Inducted into the Texas Trail of Fame in recognition of his significant contribution to the Western way of life. Bronze inlaid markers on the walkway of the Fort Worth Stockyards National Historic District honor Red along with such other inductees as Gene Autry, Charles Goodnight, Quanah Parker, and Roy Rogers.

1993

Inducted into the Colorado Country Music Hall of Fame in Colorado Springs, Colorado.
Inducted into the Hall of Great Westerners at the National Cowboy and

Western Heritage Museum in Oklahoma City. The men and women honored within the Hall of Great Westerners represent the heart and spirit of Western heritage and include such notables as Will Rogers, Teddy Roosevelt, Charles Goodnight, and Charles Russell. Explorers, Native American leaders, writers, poets, statesmen, and others who have revered the land, cherished freedom of individuality, inspired their fellow man, and found the strength of character to overcome tremendous adversity find a home within this unique and enduring national memorial.

2004
Inducted into the Texas Cowboy Hall of Fame and was the recipient of the prestigious Spirit of Texas Award.

2005
Named the 2006 Poet Laureate for the State of Texas by the Texas Commission on the Arts. He was honored in Austin before both the House of Representatives and the Senate. He is also the official Cowboy Poet Laureate of the City of San Juan Capistrano, California.
Inducted into the Texas Rodeo Cowboy Hall of Fame.

2006
Presented a membership into the Southern Legends Entertainment and Performing Arts Hall of Fame.
Inducted into the Western Music Hall of Fame.
Presented with the Charles Goodnight Award, which is presented each year to an individual, group, or institution that personifies the ideals of the Old West and has made noteworthy contributions to the preservation of the Western Heritage that has meant so much to the economy and culture of Fort Worth and all of Texas.

2007
Inducted into America's Old Time Country Music Hall of Fame in Missouri Valley, Iowa.
Inducted into the Texas Country Music Hall of Fame and Tex Ritter Museum in Carthage, Texas.
Inducted into the National Cowboys of Color Museum and Hall of Fame in Fort Worth, Texas.

2008
Inducted into the Texas Heritage Songwriters Hall of Fame in Austin, Texas.

2009
Launched television show *In the Bunkhouse with Red Steagall*, which ran on RFD-TV for four years. That show was replaced by *Red Steagall Is Somewhere West of Wall Street*, which runs on RFD-TV and The Cowboy Channel.

2011
Recipient of the Charles M. Russell Heritage Award from the Charles M. Russell Museum in Great Falls, Montana.

2012
Presented with the Boss of the Plains Award from the National Ranching Heritage Center in Lubbock, Texas. Created in 1999 and named for Stetson's premier Western hat, the award recognizes individuals who are highly regarded in their professions and who have provided noteworthy support for the National Ranching Heritage Center.

2015
Recipient of the W. A. "Bill" King Award for Excellence in Agriculture, which is presented by the Fort Worth Farm & Ranch Club and recognizes a business, individual, or family that has significantly contributed to agriculture or to the agribusiness industry.

2016
Named the Western Swing Monthly Man of the Year by *Western Swing Monthly* newsletter. It was presented "for his stellar and exemplary Western lifestyle, his distinct vocals and Western swing phrasing, and for being the role model our nation has long sought."

2018
Recipient of the Golden Spur Award from the National Ranching Heritage Center.
Named as *Western Horseman* magazine's Man of the Year.

2019
Inducted into the Texas Literary Hall of Fame.

2020
Honored as the South Texan of the Year.

2023
Named by the Professional Rodeo Cowboys Association as the 2023 PRCA Legend of Pro Rodeo.
Presented the Lifetime Achievement Award by the National Cowboy and Western Heritage Museum in Oklahoma City. This award is that institution's highest award.
Presented the Rodeo Western Heritage Award by the Amarillo Tri-State Fair.

Music and Media Awards

Red Steagall's music has been the winner of nine Western Heritage Awards from the National Cowboy and Western Heritage Museum in Oklahoma City. Western Heritage Awards honor individuals who have made significant contributions to Western heritage through creative works in literature, music, television, and film that share the great stories of the American West.

1993
Best Original Music for Warner Western album *Born to This Land*.

1995
Best Original Music for Warner Western album *Faith and Values*.

1997
Best Original Music for Warner Western album *Dear Mama, I'm a Cowboy*.

1999
Best Traditional Music for Warner Western album *Love of the West*.

2002
Best Traditional Music for Western Jubilee album *Wagon Tracks*.

2006
Best Original Music for Wildcatter Records song "How Green Was the Grazin' Back Then," from the album *The Wind, the Wire and the Rail.*

2008
Best Original Music for Wildcatter Records song "Dawson Legate," from the album *Here We Go Again* album.

2009
Best Original Composition for "A Cowboy's Special Christmas," from the Christmas CD *A Cow Camp Christmas.*

2020
Best Original Western Composition for "Hats Off to the Cowboy" from the album of the same title.

Other Western Heritage Awards include those won in the film and television division. *Red Steagall Is Somewhere West of Wall Street* has won the Western Lifestyle Program category five times: 2015, 2016, 2018, 2021, and 2022.
At the 2004 Grammy awards, Ray Charles's last album, *Genius Loves Company*, received the Grammy for Album of the Year. A song on that album, "Here We Go Again," cowritten by Red Steagall and recorded by Ray Charles and Norah Jones, won a Grammy for best record.

Books

Ride for the Brand (Texas Christian University Press, 1993) is a 168-page collection of poetry and songs embracing the Western lifestyle. The book includes lead sheets and is illustrated by Cowboy Artists of America members Bill Owen, Fred Fellows, Joe Beeler, and Howard Terpning.
The Fence That Me and Shorty Built (2001) is a 142-page collection of poems and songs, including lead sheets.
Born to This Land (2003) is a collection of poetry combined with black-and-white photographs from Pulitzer Prize–winning photographer Skeeter Hagler.
Cowboy Corner Conversations (McMurray University's State House Press, 2004) is a collection of *Cowboy Corner* radio show interviews with folks who play or have played a major part in preserving and perpetuating the history, traditions,

heritage, and values of the Western way of life.

Special Event

Each year since 1991, except during the Covid epidemic in 2020, Red Steagall has hosted the Red Steagall Cowboy Gathering and Western Swing Festival in the Stockyards National Historic District of Fort Worth, Texas. This authentic Western event, which draws thousands each year, features a ranch rodeo, chuck-wagon cookoff, youth poetry contest, youth fiddle contest, youth chuckwagon cookoff, Western swing dances, cowboy music and poetry, a trappings show, and a cattle dog challenge.

Red Steagall Discography

(Compiled by Achim Gutbrod)

LP-TAPE-CD/LABEL	TITLE	YEAR
LP/Capitol	*Party Dolls and Wine*	1972
LP/Capitol	*Somewhere My Love*	1973
LP/Capitol	*If You've Got the Time*	1973
LP/Capitol	*Finer Things in Life*	1974
LP/Tape/MCA	*Lone Star Beer & Bob Wills Music*	1976
LP/Tape/MCA	*Texas Red*	1976
LP/Tape/MCA	*For All Our Cowboy Friends*	1977
LP/Tape/MCA	*Hang on Feelin'*	1978
LP/Tape/RS Records	*Cowboy Favorites*	1984
LP/Tape/Hesston	*It's Our Life*	1985
LP/Tape/MCA	*Red Steagall*	1986
Tape/MCA	*Truck Drivin' Man*	1987
Tape/RS Records	*Ride for the Brand*	1990
Tape/RS Records	*Nothin' but a Cowboy*	1992
Tape/CD/Warner	*Born to This Land*	1993
Tape/CD/Warner	*Faith and Values*	1995
Tape/CD Eagle	*Cowboy Code*	1996
Tape/CD/Warner	*Dear Mama, I'm a Cowboy*	1997
Tape/CD/Warner	*Love of the West*	1999
CD/Koch Records	*Lone Star Beer and Bob Wills Music/ For All Our Cowboy Friends*	2000
CD/Bunkhouse Press	*Wagon Tracks*	2002
CD/Wildcatter Records	*The Wind, the Wire, and the Rail*	2005
CD/Wildcatter Records	*Here We Go Again*	2006
CD/Bunkhouse Press	*Cow Camp Christmas*	2008
CD/Bunkhouse Press	*Dreamin' of When the Grass Was Still Deep*	2011
CD/Bunkhouse Press	*Classic Red Steagall*	2014
CD/Bunkhouse Press	*Hats Off to the Cowboy*	2019

ABOUT THE AUTHORS

Red Steagall's entertainment career has covered a period of more than half a century and has spanned the globe from Australia to the Middle East, South America, and the Far East. He has performed for heads of state including President Reagan at the White House in 1983. A native Texan, Red enjoyed a career in agricultural chemistry after graduating from West Texas A&M University with a degree in animal science and agronomy. He then became a music industry executive in Hollywood and has spent the last nearly sixty years as a recording artist, songwriter, and television and motion picture personality. He currently ranches outside Fort Worth, Texas, where in addition to his entertainment activities, he is involved in numerous horse-related pursuits.

Jim Jennings lives in Amarillo, Texas, and is the retired executive director of publications for the American Quarter Horse Association. He writes the scripts for *Red Steagall Is Somewhere West of Wall Street* and has written the books *Best Remudas* and *They Still Ride Good Horses*.